# THE BEST LITTLE TOWN IN FLORIDA

## PALM BEACH SHORES, FLORIDA

# THE BEST LITTLE TOWN IN FLORIDA

## PALM BEACH SHORES, FLORIDA

## TOM MILLS

BOOK DIVISION

©2006 Tom Mills

All rights reserved. No part of this publication may be reproduced, stored in any retrieval system, or transmitted in any form or by any means, electronic, mechanical, photocopying, recording or otherwise, without the prior written permission of the copyright owner, except in the case of brief quotations embodied in critical articles and reviews.

StarGroup International, Inc.
West Palm Beach, Florida

FIRST EDITION

Edited by Shawn McAllister
Book & Cover Design by Mel Abfier

Designed and produced by StarGroup International, Inc.
(561) 547-0667
www.stargroupinternational.com

Library of Congress Cataloging-in-Publication Data pending
The Best Little Town in Florida
ISBN 1-884886-83-3

## About the Author

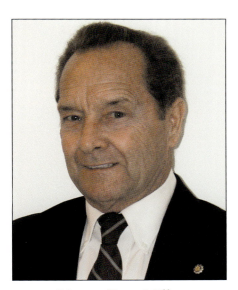

Mayor Tom Mills

Tom Mills, born and raised in the suburb of East York outside Toronto, Ontario, Canada, joined Kenting Aviation right out of school and traveled throughout North and South America conducting Airborne Geophysical Surveys. In 1963 he migrated to California where he worked for Fairchild Semiconductors in the early days of "Silicon Valley." He was pirated away along with other engineering personnel by the start up ITT Semiconductors located in West Palm Beach, Florida. His career highlights include Engineering, Engineering Management and Senior Marketing positions culminating with the position of World Wide Marketing Manager for ITT Semiconductors and then Vice-President and Director of Marketing for the Electromotive Corporation. When the company's relocation policy moved his family to temporary lodging on Singer Island, he began a longstanding love affair with the island.

In 1975 Tom brought his boat into the Cannonsport Marina. Although he was told he could stay for only two weeks, he remained for almost thirty years. He purchased the business in 1979 and only left when he sold the marina in 2004. The marina was a true family business with wife Joan opening at seven every morning, son Russell building and rebuilding the dock and motel apartments, daughter Pam taking care of reservations and sales, and her sister Linda keeping the books. In later years grandsons Daniel and Bill joined the team while they attended school.

He was recruited to join the Palm Beach Shores Volunteer Fire Department almost immediately upon his arrival in town. He answered calls for 14 years, serving in many capacities including Assistant Chief.

Appointed to the Town Commission of Palm Beach Shores in 1980 he was asked to run for mayor in 1982 and served in that capacity for two terms. In 2000 he was again approached and convinced to run again. At the completion of his current term, he will be tied for the title as the longest serving mayor (12 years) in the town's history.

The highlight of his mayoral career was being chosen as one of six finalists for Florida's Mayor of the Year award in 2004.

Tom coined the phrase, "Best Little Town in Florida," when he first was elected to head up the town commission in 1982, which has since become the town's official logo. He says that the phrase completely sums up his feelings about Palm Beach Shores.

# Contents

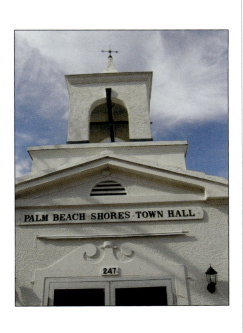

| | |
|---|---|
| xi | Foreword |
| xiii | Preface |
| xv | Acknowledgements |
| 1 | Introduction |
| 2 | Singer |
| 6 | Edwards |
| 14 | MacArthur |
| 28 | People |
| 32 | Police Department |
| 42 | Fire Department |
| 50 | Fire Department Ladies Auxilary |
| 52 | Chain Gang |
| 54 | Property Owners |
| 56 | Seasiders |
| 62 | Singer Island Business Association |
| 68 | Singer Island Civic Association |
| 70 | Old Bastards |
| 72 | Colonnades |
| 82 | Buildings |
| 90 | Auto Races |
| 98 | Peanut Island |
| 106 | Inlet |
| 116 | Sewers |
| 122 | Marinas and Lakes |
| 132 | Parks |
| 136 | Events |
| 144 | Hisory 1940s |
| 154 | View from Town Hall |
| 154 |     1950s |
| 158 |     1960s |
| 159 |     1970s |
| 166 |     1980s |
| 167 |     1990s |
| 169 |     2000+ |

x

## Foreword

### Palm Beach Shores

A paradise of a place…Palm Beach Shores is known as The Best Little Town In Florida. This paradise is both a gift of nature and a calculated creation of determined neighbors. Being surrounded by water on three sides makes this petite peninsula an attractive destination to boaters and beach bathers. The very nature of this paradise is to welcome vacationers and travelers with open arms. You will never meet a stranger in Palm Beach Shores.

Notwithstanding her attractiveness as a tropical hideaway, Palm Beach Shores is first and foremost a hometown heaven. A town created and nurtured with uncompromising care. The inclusion and participation of citizen volunteers is the core secret to this treasure of a town. Neighbors have stood shoulder to shoulder as volunteer fire fighters, stood side by side as first line responders to mother natures' fiercest storms, and generously shared and exchanged tools and talent to design and build town parks, streetscapes and a community center.

Palm Beach Shores is a small town with a huge heart. The biggest heart of all belongs to Mayor Tom Mills who has carefully assembled the pictorial history and related stories gathered within this book. Tom is the lead architect and champion of this peaceful paradise. He provides us here a glimpse of the creation and history of a town which for over fifty years has offered respite and renewal for the human spirit.

Appreciate the care Tom exercised in bringing these stories back to life and you will find it profound that the very purpose of this treasured look at our past is to provide resources to assist in the shaping of our future. Proceeds of this book will be deployed to construct a new community center for the town. So enjoy this look back with Tom and be certain that you are once again participating, just as neighbors do, in the ongoing creation of this paradise we know as Palm Beach Shores…
The Best Little Town in Florida.

Senator Jeff Atwater

## Preface

No one is more responsible for the Town of Palm Beach Shores becoming "The Best Little Town in Florida" than Tom Mills. This wonderfully unique community of 1200 residents, situated on the southern tip of Singer Island and surrounded by water on three sides, manages — largely due to Tom's efforts — to retain the ambiance and natural charm of a small secluded town, despite being located in the highly developed area of South Florida.

Tom's love affair with the town began in 1979, when he and his family settled in the town as the new owners of Cannonsport Marina. His civic involvement began soon thereafter with various volunteer activities, including Volunteer Firefighter, and continued with his election to the Town Commission in 1981, and then as Mayor for two terms. For the next fifteen years, his civic activities centered on professional and service associations, earning him numerous "Man of the Year" and other presitgious awards. Then, in the year 2000, Tom was elected Mayor again, and orchestrated the much needed upgrade of the town's infrastructure which continues as of this writing, well into Tom's third consecutive mayoral term.

Who, better then, to produce this pictorial history of the town? Tom's unique perspective as a local citizen, business owner, elected Commissioner and Mayor over nearly three decades is reflected in this delightful book. Enjoy!

William Hayes, former Vice-Mayor of Palm Beach Shores

# Acknowledgements

A history of the Town has been my "one day I'll do it" project that started in 1980. Reading old meeting minutes and newspaper clippings got me interested and the history booklet written by Anita Redding and her committee in 1976 just whetted my appetite for more details. In 2003, I attempted to put some time aside each day to coalesce the thousands of pieces of information I had collected over the intervening 23 years. The deeper I delved the more details I found. I finally decided to quit looking and start writing while I still had time!

I found some discrepancies in previous works and worked overtime to get at the truth. Most facts stated have been double checked when possible, but the usual disclaimer is made.

I would like to acknowledge the many, many who when they heard of my project sent price lists, postcards, brochures and other memorabilia. Apparently I am not the only collector in town.

The Town Hall staff, Sue Franklin; Roberta Loftus, Carolyn Gangwer, Cindy Lindskoog have all been both helpful and supportive. Thanks.

But, the main reason writing the book was possible is because I was allowed to spend the countless hours at Town Hall. That came about because Joan, with our kids help, agreed to run the family business (Cannonsport Marina and Resort). Russell, Linda and Pamela proceeded to prove that I was not really needed. With the additional help of grandsons Danny and Bill the business continued to flourish and actually produced bigger numbers without me being around.

Collecting the photos and writing my thoughts have been the easy part. Making it all come together is a job for the professionals and I certainly found the right ones. StarGroup International under the leadership of Brenda Star, the editing of Shawn McAllister and the graphic work of Mel Abfier has been just amazing. Thanks guys!

## Introduction

The idea of compiling a photo history of Palm Beach Shores is a very personal vision that was undertaken solely as an individual project. Other than the use of the town purchased computer in my office at Town Hall, there was no taxpayer dollars used directly or indirectly in the preparation of this book.

The expenses have been my own with some assistance given to help underwrite the cost of publication. It is hoped that production costs will be recovered from sales. Nevertheless, I have pledged to contribute 10% of all sales to the town's new Community Center.

The history of the area is not ancient by any means. Seminoles lived in a seaside village at Jupiter and on the mainland nearby (destroyed by the U.S. Army's Captain Wade in 1841). It would not be a stretch to suppose that some of the more elite migrated to the town site to be a little closer to the future affluence of Palm Beach. Since there is not an archeology society on the island, it cannot be confirmed who first discovered this little tropical paradise.

Settlers were few and far between. The man who is regarded as the first white area resident was Mr. August Lang (see Inlet chapter) who arrived in the 1850s long before those who deserted here from both sides of the Civil War along with runaway slaves and commercial fishermen drawn by the proximity of the Gulf Stream waters.

Palm Beach Shores and Singer Island emerged after Flagler developed his Royal Poinciana hotel in Palm Beach. The island, accessible only by boat, sat isolated and unused for many years except for picnickers, and fishermen squatters. One of these visitors was Mr. Paris Singer. A good place to start our story of Palm Beach Shores' history would be with Mr. Singer and his shenanigans.

# Singer

From the beginning of the 20th Century, Flagler's Palm Beach grew, attracting the elite from all over North America and Europe. The mainland grew both as the necessary support for Palm Beach and independently. With the dredging of the inlet at its present location, expansion of coastline development was curtailed to the north and expansion was directed to the ample prime waterfront land to the south.

A land boom in South Florida was in full swing in the early 1920s. Many small investors were successful by putting a few dollars down and flipping their purchase at a great profit before making their first payment. The same

*Singer Island Bridge 1935. The bridge was rebuilt in 1935 after a hurricane in 1926 made the old one unusable. With the end of the land real estate boom, a bigger 1928 storm and the depression, there was no demand for the immediate rebuilding of Singer's 1925 structure.*

thing is happening at the turn of the 21st Century.

Isaac Singer made his fortune with his sewing machine companies. In addition to his reputation for business success, he also had a well deserved reputation of making babies. He was the proud father of 24 children. The 23rd was a boy named Paris, after the city where he was born. Paris lived in Europe most of his life and helped spend the family fortune building hospitals in England and France during the First World War. He had a relationship with Isadora Duncan, the "ahead of her time" feminist dancer known as the originator of the modern dance. He sponsored her dance school in France and fathered her son Patrick. He reportedly followed Isadora to Palm Beach around 1917. He blended with the "in" crowd and liked the life so much that he purchased a home. He met architect Addison Mizner and the two became friends and business partners. Singer had Mizner draw up plans for a military hospital in Palm Beach, but the war ended and the building was turned into the Everglades Social Club. Singer and Mizner collaborated on many Palm Beach projects and much of the layout of streets and the design of the downtown areas are results of this collaboration.

Mizner's successes are still easily identified by his unique style. Examples of his work can be found all over Palm Beach County, especially in Boca Raton.

The island had no access, except by boat, and consisted of a desolate scrub interior with a beautiful beach. Singer would bring his friends to picnic on the beach and he often dreamed of creating a private resort that would rival the best of Palm Beach. In 1924 Paris decided to make his ideas a reality. He had Mizner design two hotels for his Shangri-La. He envisioned a tunnel or bridge connecting his island to Palm Beach, but this idea was shot down by all the local authorities.

His hastily contrived plans contained lots of big picture material, but lacked details. He planned on building one hotel on the north end of the island and one to the south. Between the two would be a fabulous 36 hole golf course. The hotel to the north was to be called the Blue Heron and the southern one the Paris Singer. The Blue Heron was to be the most luxurious in the country with suites going for $300 per night while the Paris Singer was to be a full amenity resort. The Duchess of Richelieu was contracted to design the interior.

The sales plan called for subdividing the island into three sections. Each section was then broken down into small lots. By selling one section at a time at land boom prices, the cost for the hotel development would be covered. The idea was to sell a section and then to raise the price. The sales plan proceeded before the existing lots were under Singer's control.

The first section sold out so quickly that the real estate agent changed the agreed upon plan and sold the other two sections as well. Unfortunately, all were sold for a great price, but with only a $250 binder. On paper, money was made, but not much financing was raised. The hotel was scheduled to open in 1926-27, but guests needed a way to get on the island. The county agreed to build a bridge if Mr. Singer would float the bond. He did and then purchased all the bonds himself. The Sherman Point Bridge was built in 1925 at the narrowest point of the lake separating the island from the mainland. The wooden structure, sitting on wood pilings, provided year round access to what became known as Singer's Island.

"The best laid plans oft times…." in Singer's case did go wrong. Clear title to the entire island was just not available. Many parcels had been previously sold and records were not always easily obtained. Very few second payments were made and almost no third payments. Singer condensed the plan and temporarily eliminated the northern most hotel and golf course. He went ahead with the southernmost hotel, but changed the name to the Blue Heron. The anticipated opening was scheduled for 1927. Singer's buddy Mizner designed the hotel, but Singer was in such a hurry he proceeded with the plans still on the drafting table. Instead of filling and compressing the building site, pilings were driven and sand later pumped under the floor. The service wing was finished and the rest of the building well underway before the plug was pulled. Some say it was halted by Singer's mother, who stopped the cash infusion when expenditures reached the $2 million mark. Dinnerware, silverware and linens with the hotel name embossed had already arrived and had to be stored in a rented warehouse. Bond and mortgage troubles, followed by litigation, stopped all talk of any contingency plan being possible.

Then the 1926 hurricane wiped out the bridge and the local Great Florida Land Boom bubble burst. Talk was heard of new financing, but another hurricane in 1928 caused all speculators to shy away from South Florida followed by the whole country settling into the Great Depression and the project came to a standstill. The island went back to the isolated state it had always been in, with the exception that it now had a seven-story skeleton building on the beach that the locals called Singer's Folly.

Even though a boy fell to his death while playing in the building in 1935, the hotel stood until 1940. That's when what was anticipated to be the "grandest of all hotels," the Blue Heron, was finally demolished.

Paris returned to his homestead in Torbay England and in 1929 converted it into a country club. He suffered from poor health

*Singer's Hotel. Pictured shortly after construction stopped in 1927. Known as Singer's Folly, it was eventually torn down in 1940.*

including insomnia, which he unsuccessfully tried to cure with a relaxing Nile River vacation. He spent the rest of his life commuting between his home in France and London where he died in 1931. He is buried in the family plot in England.

*Paris Singer*

Reproduced by kind permission of Torbay Library Service.

# Edwards

A.O. (Alfred Octavius) Edwards, the "Father of Palm Beach Shores," was a man who had the exceptional foresight and fortitude to visualize and then to transform the south end of a desolate barrier island with the dedication and planning needed to create "the Best Little Town in Florida."

After World War II the country was not made up of the transitory population that we know today. Since then we have had three generations of families ready to pick up and move across the country for a better job. In 1947 the thoughts of the men and women returning after months away in the service were about a return to their roots, family and to what they had left behind. Edwards believed that there was enough local families, servicemen who had served or recuperated in the area, and seniors from up north who could afford a second home. He hedged his bet by planning a complete community that included mom and pop style tourist apartments and a well designed shopping center. This created a market for young families, retirees, future retirees, shop keepers, and those who wanted the good life but still needed an income. The location of each activity was rigorously controlled by restrictions and covenants that in some cases remained unchanged when they later became the town's code of ordinances. Times were different. Homes were not an easy sell. There were still many lots sitting empty in the late '60s.

*A.O. Edwards*
*Photo used in 1947 ads for the new Palm Beach Shores development*

Mr. Edwards was born on April 28, 1876 in the Town of Ripley, Derbyshire, England, which is about 150 miles northwest of London. He became an engineer and studied railroad construction under Sir Robert Elliot Cooper. Sir Elliot Cooper was the recognized authority in this field of engineering at the time. The first project for A.O. was rebuilding some of the devastated areas of southern France. Next, he built a 200-mile long railroad in India through terrain described as mostly dense jungle. These accomplishments resulted in him achieving worldwide peer recognition.

He returned to England and concentrated on commercial building construction, specifically hotels in the London area. He rebuilt the famed Savoy and built the Mayfair Hotel, which still has a five-star rating. He then designed, engineered and built the largest hotel in Europe …the Grosvenor House on London's Park Lane.

Lord Chetwynd was the first to build on the land on which the hotel is located, which later became home to the son of King George II and then the brother of King George III. In 1806 the property was purchased by Lord Grosvenor and the homestead named Grosvenor House. The last Grosvenor was made the Duke of Westminster in 1874 by Queen Victoria.

Mr. Edwards bought the property and began construction of his hotel in 1927. Not all Londoners were impressed. He used American construction methods and designs, prompting one letter to the editor of the London Times that described the results as "an insult to the good taste and aesthetic judgement of the citizens of the metropolis." The hotel opened in May 1929 with all the glitz and glamour expected and ironically has been looked upon as a bastion of good taste and aesthetic quality.

The Grosvenor House project tells a lot about Mr. Edwards. For starters he was an avid ice skater and incorporated the Grosvenor Ice Rink into what is now the Great Room of the hotel. The rink was the home of the Park Lane Ice Club. The hotel rink closed in 1935. Since then thousands of people have enjoyed their functions in the room without ever guessing that the ice-making apparatus and pipes are still

*Ariel view of Grosvenor House Hotel. Some believe the building design intentionally spells "A. O." as in A.O. Edwards.*

in place below their feet. The Great Room is still today the largest hotel banquet space in Europe.

During World War II the great room was used as an Officers Club hosting more than 300,000 officers from allied forces. It served as a U.S. Officer's Mess from 1943 through the end of the war. During this time 5,500,000 meals were served. Today the room hosts elaborate social affairs and is renowned for the annual Arts and Antique Fair (originated in 1934). Mr. Edwards marketed his hotel primarily to trans-Atlantic steamboat passengers. These travelers were accustomed to a very high level of service and his hotel was designed to fit in with this expectation. He opened an office on Fifth Avenue in New York to better serve his clientele. His success is shown by the list of those who have used his Grosvenor House, such as Orson Welles, Jacqueline Onassis, Henry Kissinger, General Dwight D. Eisenhower, General George Patton, Sammy Davis Jr., Muhammed Ali, and Ella Fitzgerald.

Mr. Edwards also developed the Queens Court area of London, in which he also included a competition ice rink. The Queens Court rink is still going strong after 75 years and has the distinction of being the oldest ice rink in the country. It is the home ice of the Queens Ice Dance Club and the only ice rink in central London. Due to its long narrow shape it has never been a championship rink, but it certainly has produced its share of local, British, World and Olympic champions. A woman named Gladys Hogg (MBE) who coached continuously from the day the rink opened in 1930 until her retirement in 1984 is given credit for the success of so many champions from such a small rink.

The Grosvenor House Hotel also brought

*Great Room of Grovsvenor Hotel is still today the largest hotel banquet room in Europe.*

*Ad for Ice Rink located in 'Great Room' from 1929-35.*

*1950's formal portrait of A.O. Edwards with ever present cigar.*

out the entrepreneur in Edwards in an unusual advertising gimmick that paid off in a big way.

The attempts to set long distance flight records in the 1930s had the attention of the whole world. To promote the centennial of the City of Melbourne and the State of Victoria in Australia, a race from London to Melbourne was proposed. Australian candy maker Sir MacPherson Robertson agreed to put up the prize money ($50,000 first prize) and the race was on.

*Edwards Ice Rink in Queen Court, London.*

England did not have a fast, long distance aircraft in production. When it looked like the race may go to the KLM Royal Dutch entry that planned to enter the brand new, American-made Douglas DC-2, the De Havilland Aircraft Company announced that they would build a contender if they could find three buyers.  Mr. Edwards stepped up to plate (or wicket) and placed an order.

The race, now known officially as the MacRobertson Air Race, was scheduled for October 20, 1934. Mr. Edwards placed his order the end of February, giving De Havilland seven month to design, build, test and deliver a state-of-the-art aircraft. The challenge was met with the first of three "Comets" taking to the air in September test flights. Mr. Edwards' aircraft did not receive its Certificate of Airworthiness until October the 9th. The night before the race it was decided that the Comet's oil tanks must be enlarged, so De Havilland crews worked all night to have the three sleek, aircraft on the starting line modified and ready to go. One stood out with its crimson and silver color scheme, and sporting the name along the fuselage in big letters… Grosvenor House.

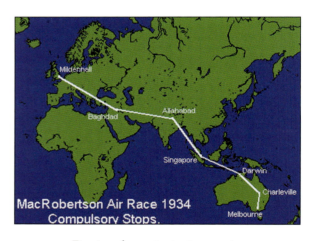

*Route of greatest air race in aviation history.*

Of the original 64 entries, 20 actually lined up at the starting line for what was described by Time Magazine as the "greatest air race in aviation history." At 6:30 am Sir Alfred Bower, the acting Lord Mayor of London, signaled the start and more than 60,000 spectators cheered.   After flying 11,323 miles, the

Grosvenor House set down in Melbourne, Australia a little under three days later — seventy one hours, one minute and three seconds later to be exact — to the roar of a crowd of more than 100,000 well wishers. If the name of Mr. Edwards' hotel had been unknown to any one before the race, Grosvenor House was now a household name. Mr. Edwards sold his hotel the next year.

The original Grosvenor House Comet aircraft is airworthy today and kept at London's Old Warden Airport as part of the Shuttleworth Collection. A replica was built in 1991-92 in Riverside California and is on display at the Wings of History Museum at Watsonville Municipal Airport. The original aircraft set a London to Cape Town and return record in 1937 and in 1938 set a record for England to New Zealand and Australia to New Zealand.

These latter two records were not broken until 1945 and 1946. The Comet was a streamline design utilizing plywood on a spruce frame, covered in fabric. This inexpensive manufacturing technique was later duplicated to create one of World War II's finest aircraft, De Havilland's famous Mosquito fighter.

A.O. then directed his interest to Cape Town, South Africa. He started a finance company, the Inter-Union Finance Company, and developed a portion of Cape Town at the foot of Table Mountain. Another of his interests came to light in South Africa … love of auto racing. The South African Auto Union was a struggling organization but had potential championship drivers. They later excelled in major European races. What was missing was a professional racing circuit. Mr. Edwards purchased land in Pollsmoor south of Cape Town and built a first class racing circuit 7.5 miles long, including lots of grandstand seating. Although he had sold the Grosvenor House hotel in 1935, he named the first Grand Prix at his new race track the Grosvenor Grand Prix. It took place on January 16, 1937 with expectation of 120,000 spectators. While it was not a financial success, it did put South Africa, as a Grand Prix host, and the South African Auto Union on the map.

In 1939 Mr. Edwards moved to the United States with his wife Helene Jadwiga, a Polish Countess whom he had married in Westminster in 1936.

They bought a home in Palm Beach on South Ocean Boulevard, which they named South Winds. He was active in oil drilling ventures in Texas, Kansas and Oklahoma. He purchased and subdivided the Stotesbury Estate in Palm Beach, then purchased and develop 25 acres at the north end of Hypoluxo Island in Lantana.

A.O. became a naturalized citizen of the U.S. in 1946. About the same time the Palm Beach Post reported that Mr. Edwards had purchased 200 Acres on the southern tip of

Singer Island. The sale included 3,000 feet of prime ocean frontage, 4,000 feet of Lake waterfront property and a half mile on the inlet. The price $475,000. There had been talk of the county buying and making a county park in the area but a May 1945 bond referendum was defeated at the polls. He compared the waterfront locality to Michigan's St. Clair Shores and agreed to name his new development Palm Beach Shores after it was suggested by the wife of his attorney.

By 1947 docks were being built, roads paved, water lines put in and sales brochures printed advertising lot and home sales in Palm Beach Shores. The brochures illustrated what has to be some of the best community planning of the time. The Inlet Court Hotel was built on the ocean, (later to be named the Colonnades). Land purchased in Riviera Beach, (Blue Heron and A1A) was used for water wells, water storage and purification. Lines were run from that location across the intracoastal waterway and then to every lot in town.

A study of the original town plan is almost identical to the existing town zoning map. Larger buildings were allowed on waterfront lots around the town's perimeter (district C and D). A second area that does deviate, but for the most part utilizes the inner periphery, which allowed small apartments (district B) and the core center designated for single family homes only (district A). The actual zoning districts were drawn up to accommodate apartments that were already built.

Mr. Edwards was Chairman of the Board of Colonnades Inc., which was the holding company for his town investments. He served as the first Mayor and personally directed the town's growth until Palm Beach Shores was chartered and elections were held. His love of automobile racing once again became apparent in 1949 when he allowed the Palm Beach Grand Prix to be held on the newly paved streets of his almost empty town.

In 1954 he saw a chemical research company that he thought had great promise, Permachem Corporation, bought controlling interest and moved their lab to West Palm Beach. He concentrated on this and his other business ventures and gradually bowed out of direct involvement with municipal management after the town was chartered. He also spent more time at the many social clubs he belonged to in Palm Beach, Philadelphia, and Narragansett (Rhode Island). In 1958 Mr. Edwards suffered a stroke and could not participate in tennis competition, nor in the daily swimming that he loved. After two years of illness, he died on August 24, 1960 at his summer home "Afterall" in Villanova, Pennsylvania. He was 84 years old.

A.O. fully enjoyed life. His legacy is in the buildings he left behind that will stand for centuries, railroads that extended several countries' commerce, world records for long distance flight, race tracks that allowed major drivers to grow to world class status, and skating rinks that survived world wars and continue to provide a venue for the sport he loved. As a pinnacle to his career, he left us, the lucky ones, with an island gem, the "Best Little Town in Florida."

*De Havilland Comet named Grosvenor House. Winner of the London to Melbournes Australia Greatest Air Race.*

# MacArthur

*Mr. MacArthur always had time to feed his ducks. When guests complained of the mess the ducks made, they were invited to find other accommodations.*

If A.O. Edwards was the Father of Palm Beach Shores, the Rich Uncle would have to be John D. MacArthur. Mr. MacArthur, known to friends and business acquaintances as "John D," "Mr. Mac," or "Skipper," was the most controversial character the town ever had to contend with and he seemed to enjoy the role he played and the reputation he gained.

He was known as a gutsy, aggressive and frequently insulting individual. He had only a grade school education, but he knew what the family motto "Fide et Opera" meant, or at least he knew his interpretation ... "Be honest and work like a son of a bitch." One interviewer wrote, "He swears like a sailor in normal conversation and when he is angry he is unprintable and his grammar would give a high school teacher heart palpitations."

He was born in 1897 in the impoverished coal mining area of Pennsylvania where his dirt farmer and wandering evangelist father was passing through with his wife and their other six children. Mr. Mac persevered and at the time of his death was one of the three wealthiest men in America. The three of his brothers who reached adulthood also became highly successful in their chosen fields. Brother Alfred in insurance, Telfer in publishing and Charles as a newsman, playwright and movie screenwriter. John D also had a very famous cousin, General Douglas MacArthur.

John held numerous jobs, including newspaper copyboy for the Chicago Examiner where brother Charlie was a reporter, insurance salesman (for brother Alfred's company), and three business ventures he tried but failed at before he found a measure of independent success. He joined the U.S. Navy in World War I and then the British Royal Flying Corps. where he suffered a back injury in a crash after running out of fuel. Later he went AWOL but returned. Back in Chicago he met, wooed and married Louise Ingals before he was 23. He tried running a bakery and a gas station to support the two children that Louise had bore him in quick succession. In 1926 Mr. MacArthur switched back to selling insurance.

The marriage had problems and Louise took the children to California to live with her grandparents. John D met a pretty secretary, Catherine Hyland, who worked for his brother. A week-end trip to Mexico produced a quickie divorce and a just as quick wedding. It was many years later before his first wife agreed to a divorce. Catherine is credited with being the bookkeeper, auditor and business manager for all of MacArthur's successes. He said Bankers Life and Casualty Company of Chicago would not have been possible without her. She was his Office Manager throughout the rest of his life.

In 1928 at the age of 30 Mr. MacArthur purchased the Marquette Life Insurance Company for $7,500. The Depression soon followed and his assets shrank to $15.31. While other small insurance companies went under, Marquette stayed afloat. The Bankers Life and Casualty Company of Chicago was one of the less fortunate and was taken over by the Illinois Insurance Department. In 1935 John D borrowed $2,500 and purchased it, lock, stock and barrel. Although insurance sales were a very hard sell, Bankers succeeded by offering policies with weekly and/or monthly premium payments for change, e.g., a dollar a month would buy $108 of Bankers' life insurance. Large companies with large overheads could not compete at this level and a new market opened up.

By 1940 the company had over $1,000,000 in assets. When Mr. MacArthur died in 1978 assets had surpassed one billion dollars. The company had 5,000 agents and brokers with $5.5 billion insurance coverage in force. John D was the sole owner.

In the 1960s Mr. MacArthur's interest turned to real estate and development. His holdings included 100,000 acres of land in Florida, several development companies and shopping centers, paper and pulp companies, several publishing enterprises, hotels, radio and television stations, banks, and twelve insurance companies, as well as 19 commercial, office and apartment buildings in New York City.

His first local project was the founding of what is now the City of Palm Beach Gardens. The development was centered on a new golf club that John D was building. Not just another golf course but two (later enlarged to three) championship courses that would be the home and headquarters of the PGA. In 1964 plans for the operation of the private club were announced. They included availability of a $10 Social Membership, $6 winter and $3 summer green fees. The 55,600 square foot clubhouse was available for non-member social functions and a swimming pool was planned for the near future. Soon the best golfers in the world would be regular visitors to this private club. Some of the best known tournaments in the world were played here, including the richest at the time – the $275,000 PGA National Team Championship. In 1981 the PGA and Mr. MacArthur had a falling out. Some say the PGA left, some say Mr. Mac told them to leave. In any case although the plate glass windows overlooking the greens still were engraved with the PGA logo, the course became the JDM Country Club. When put on the market in 1987 it was valued at $80 to $100 million and the 1,300 members were paying $4,000 annual membership fees.

The need for easy access to the city was made possible by a new exit from the Florida Turnpike, financed by Mr. MacArthur. The road now led directly into the development and the PGA clubhouse, and provided a direct link to both north and south Florida. Like most of his ventures, Palm Beach Gardens was a very successful endeavor.

Besides a very extensive advertising campaign to have his Palm Beach Gardens development known, Mr. Mac knew how to get prime publicity through the news media. In 1964 the famous DeLong ruby was stolen as part of a $410,000 jewel heist from the New York Museum of Natural History. A ransom of $25,000 was demanded by the thieves. John D very publicly put up the money for the ransom. The story of the recovery and the trial of Richard Pearson was front page news and most accounts mentioned John D. MacArthur of Palm Beach Gardens and his PGA National Golf Club, although one write-up only said that John D was the brother of Charles, the movie

*Mr. MacArthur in 1965. Photo taken for article "Millionaire Takes On Small Town."*

screenwriter who was married to movie star Helen Hayes.

In 1964 Mr. Mac called in his experts to get their advice as to what he should do with the two-story Colonnades Hotel he had purchased from the A.O. Edwards estate for $800,000. The unanimous decision was to raze it. So Mr. D thanked them, proceeded to ignore his high priced advisors and poured money into the old structure for the next four years … more money, he remarked, than he could ever expect to regain from hotel operations. Frank Sinatra would be proud of John D. He did it his way. Building permits and health departments were not allowed to stand in the way of progress, nor were red tag orders or other legal actions able to stop work.

Mr. MacArthur's first step was to appear before the Town Commission and introduce himself. He said that he wanted to be a good neighbor and planned to make the Colonnades Hotel "a monument to the Town of Palm Beach Shores and to John D. MacArthur." He obtained permits to add three stories to the existing main building and to construct an additional building consisting of a two-story convention hall with hotel rooms on four upper floors. He then proceeded to build seven-story structures that had little, if any, resemblance to the permitted plans.

The Town Commission was just completing a code amendment which extended the building line on oceanfront property 100 feet closer to the ocean. Mr. MacArthur requested a special exception of an additional 100 feet. When the Commission denied his request Mr. Mac went public with his not so veiled threat to go ahead with the purchase and construction, but to let one of his tax-free foundations operate the Colonnades as a senior citizens' rest home. The implication being that the town would lose the tax income from its largest tax payer. Why the request was denied is not clear. The depth of the beach had grown immensely since the inlet was cut deeper in 1935 and continued to grow until the sand transfer plant was installed years later. There was not a coastal construction line to contend with and the Planning and Zoning board had voted unanimously to allow the request. In any case, a slab foundation was poured and a Cabana Club building was built. Years later this building was not removed when the Colonnades was demolished. It was well seaward of the, now in existence, Coastal Construction Line and, as a grandfathered structure, the foundation was used by the Marriott for a pool snack bar. Between the time when the hotel was closed and the time the other buildings were torn down, actor Burt Reynolds used the Cabana Club building as the office for his private investigator TV series "B.L. Stryker."

The second major problem came about

*When town denied John D's first variance request, he threatened to turn hotel into non taxable rest home.*

JOHN D. MACARTHUR
1001 PARK AVENUE
LAKE PARK, FLORIDA

June 14, 1968

Honorable C. J. Wolfe
Mayor, Town of Palm Beach Shores
247 Edwards Lane
Palm Beach Shores, Florida

Dear Mayor:

In the hope of saving the tax payers legal fees I am writing you the facts concerning the recent warrants served on the people working on the Colonnades parking lot.

The entire cost of the storm drain on Ocean Avenue was assessed to the property owners. The parking area, roofs and paved drives are incapable of absorbing any water and it all drains to a low spot almost in the center of the paved south parking lot. I thought it would be a good idea to run a drain, at my own expense, from the center of the lot direct to the storm sewer while the same was being installed. I wrote you, or the Building Commissioner, of my idea but the reply was that as long as I had building materials on the parking lot I would not be permitted to tie into the storm drain the property owners were obligated to pay for. I have not been able to find the letter -- perhaps I sent it to my attorney -- but I could see no relationship between building the drain and the storage of our surplus building material.

One of my employees told me the Police Department would appreciate our fencing our property because when it was wide open they had no control over tresspassers. I agreed with the suggestion and decided to reinstall the fence.

Honorable C. J. Wolfe — 2 — June 14, 196[8]

[...]et was broken up. The men were careless in view [of the] fact they knew we planned to have the entire area [paved] at our expense.

[If] the incident go to trial we will prove that we [are we]ll within our rights to install three lengths of [pipe un]der our own fence on our own property without per[mission] of the Town Commissioners.

[If th]e Commission does not agree because when we [wanted t]o plant our trees and prepare the ground on [the stre]et recently acquired south of our parking lot [as a ]fact, we must get a permit to plant trees and [it ]was nailed on the telephone pole. Our men [were phy]sically taken to the police station and they [lost] much time, so I regarded this as unimportant.

[For in]formation we have installed 2" pipe between [two] of the fence we are installing. When the [pipe is] high in the parking lot it will drain to [and] eventually find its way to the new storm [drain. It wi]ll suffice for the time being. Until [the] Building Inspector becomes more in[terested in the] efficient disposal of water during heavy [rains I will n]ot extend the proposed drain.

Very truly yours,

John MacArthur

*Letter John D. MacArthur wrote to mayor explaining why he was connecting non-permitted lines to town's storm sewer. He was accused of using similar connections for septic tank run-off.*

when John D applied for and received a permit to install a boiler to heat water for the hotel kitchen. He later tried, on three occasions, to modify the permit to include an incinerator. These requests were repeatedly denied. After the boiler went into operation, neighbors started to complain about the black smoke and foul odors emanating from the hotel. A commissioner joined the building inspector and the Police Chief to perform an unannounced visit to the kitchen and remove a bucket of ashes from the hot water boiler, complete with steak bones, citrus rinds, and other partially burnt food stuff.

The incinerator incident marked the end of MacArthur's permit application days. The good neighbor policy no longer existed and the situation became, as one source said, a confrontation between "implacable hostility on one hand and scarcely-veiled defiance on the other." In the next few years more than two dozen warrants were issued for violations at the hotel. Many ended up in court, whether it was in the town's Municipal Court or the District and Appellate Courts.

The most serious violation concerned the old septic tank system not being able to handle the sewage from the new additional rooms. Illegal pipes leading to a storm sewer were installed and also to the swimming pool drain that went directly to the beach and ocean. The stench coming from the storm sewers and the overflowing tanks of raw sewage once again had citizens up in arms. Eventually the problem was fixed by connecting hotel sewer lines to the City of Riviera Beach system via a lift station. Apparently some bathrooms were not connected since continual complaints were still being received for many, many years up until the time the hotel was demolished.

The open hostilities and most serious confrontations ended with the completion of the hotel construction, but not before a very sad episode took place.

On the night of January 28, 1968, Mr. MacArthur showed up in Town Hall, where the town's Municipal Court was held, to answer 20 charges of code violations. He was fully loaded for battle, having four defense lawyers and his own court reporter accompanying him. The trial started at 7 p.m. with a full house of spectators including one of Mac's severest critics… Mayor Robert McBrien. The trial dragged on and by 10 p.m. the court reporter requested a break. Judge Billy R. Jackson declared a brief recess. MacArthur decided he had had enough for the night and proceeded to leave. The mayor, sitting in the back row, protested that Mac was the defendant and was under subpoena and could not leave. "Can't I?" was the reply, "Watch me!" The trial resumed with no official notice of the defendant's absence. It was still in progress at 11:30 p.m.

when Mayor McBrien suffered a heart attack, keeled over and died.

Town Attorney Angus Campbell publicly stated that the 20 charges were just a first shot in a war the town intended to win. He said that MacArthur should obey the law like everyone else.

"What's the difference between him and any other citizen?" he asked.

The answer was, "Almost a billion dollars."

Before completion of the Colonnades Hotel, MacArthur moved into a relatively small apartment on the top floor of the Ballroom building. It was described as being thrown together by a color blind interior decorator. The rug was a greenish yellow, walls were painted a somber green, the ceiling had a bright blue and green checkerboard design. The apartment did not face the ocean, just the opposite in fact. The view was of the hotel parking lot. Yet it was from here that he and wife Catherine handled the finances of their expansive financial empire. MacArthur still took time once a year to visit his sales force at Bankers Insurance. His personal appearances were timed to bonuses and sales commissions presentations. He would let his sales team know he was still one of the boys and he would give a little inspirational talk.

He conducted day by day affairs from his famous table in the coffee shop on the hotel's main floor. With his ever-present cigarette in his mouth, he would field one telephone call after another and meet the lucky few who he wanted to see. You could wait for hours and never get a chance to say hello if you were not one of the chosen few.

Mr. Mac became known as an eccentric. It was a label he cherished and encouraged. His dress was such that he was mistaken for the maintenance man more than once and in one instance actually went along with a woman who wanted a bellhop to carry her bags up to her room. He just picked them up and deposited them in the room and cheerfully accepted her tip! He flew tourist class and said he met a lot of nice people that way; he drove a seven-year-old automobile and he openly disliked the society members of Palm Beach.

His personification of a good old boy was sometimes to excess. He would answer reporters' questions with statements they didn't expect. He told the New York Times that he still enjoyed pinching females. Later he halfheartedly denied the statement, but put himself deeper in the hole he dug by saying, "Patting an ass is just like shaking hands these days." And saying "I never had an affair worthy of the name, although I have snuck around a little, as any man would admit he's done if he's honest."

He had absolutely no time for Big Brother government and said he could never have been successful if he had to operate under the present day bureaucracy.

"The liberals have destroyed what makes this country great," he said. "Now the government is telling everybody how to run his business, how much to pay people, and how long they should work."

In 1971 MacArthur suffered a serious bout of viral pneumonia and was told he might not return from Good Samaritan Hospital. He ended up staying, in and out of intensive care, for four months. He started bleeding and doctors operated to find the cause. The malignant tumor they removed encompassed one half of his stomach. Without the hospital stay with the pneumonia, the chances are the cancer would not have been detected before it was too late to operate. Mr. Mac chalked it up to "MacArthur Luck."

With construction of the hotel complete, many problems went away. The Property Owners Association convinced him to play Santa Claus at a kid's Christmas program and later gave him an Honorary Lifetime Membership.

Once he was on the mend he reverted to his true character and demanded his release. The doctor told him he had to stay to be near the oxygen and the monitoring equipment, etc., to which Mr. Mac said he would buy it all. He did. He bought everything from electrocardiogram machines to the hospital bed. After the deal was made, a poor nurse who was unaware of the agreement told MacArthur that he would not be leaving for a while. He went on a rampage using a chair to break windows and threatening to jump in order to leave. Finally help arrived. The head nurse assured everyone that Mr. Mac was indeed leaving in the morning. MacArthur's understated reply was, "They were probably pretty glad to see me go."

If John D's coffee table was his best known trademark, his second best would be his ever-increasing flock of ducks. In the 1960s someone deposited thirteen ducklings in the hotel decorative lagoon. Guests thought they were very cute and enjoyed feeding them. Later Easter ducklings were added and then a few wild mallards and wild geese joined the throng. Eventually this group intermixed and John D had 100 of his fowl friends fouling up the pool, the grass, and the walkways around the hotel, as well as the carpeting inside the hotel. Guests complained, staff complained, but to no avail. Mr. Mac enjoyed them and would feed them daily. He did prune back the flock by depositing some at the Indian Hammock Preserve near Fort Drum on a regular basis. Mr. Mac insured they would have a safe home before letting them go. He also smiled that perverse smile when leading some sales person to the coffee table via a roundabout way that included stepping lightly or else.

With all the quirks and bad boy antics of Mr. Mac, it is only fair to present the positives, which as far as the town and surrounding communities are concerned, far outweigh any long term damage he may have caused with his shenanigans.

His first major development, Palm Beach Gardens, and the PGA Golf and Country Club were immediate successes. The Gardens became the "in" place for upper and middle management, engineering and accounting personnel. MacArthur gets credit for bringing many of the high technology companies moving into the north county at the time. Included were R.C.A., Pratt and Whitney Aircraft, Sikorsky Helicopters, ITT Semiconductors, Honeywell Semiconductors, Solitron Semiconductors, RCA Computers and Phillips Components. Considering that MacArthur built the water plant and all the other necessary infrastructure, the freeway interchange, and rewarded builders to get the first homes built,

*1967 view of hotel expansion. Growing from two to seven stories without benefits of proper permits.*

he must be given credit for turning a snake infested wilderness into a desirable town in a matter of a few years. The city has never stopped growing and today property values attest to its popularity and success.

MacArthur had his soft side that is not as well known. His acts of charity were carried out anonymously. The caring attitude he had for his employees brought about fierce loyalty and it seemed everyone had a story about his stepping in to help when an employee's family member was ailing. And, of course, he loved his ducks!

In the sixties he tried to lure Disney to Palm Beach County instead of Orlando. He created a wild animal refuge west of the B-Line Highway that included tigers, lions and bears. Many movie and TV series productions used the site, with the most famous being the TV show "Gentle Ben."

*Although he was in constant battle with environmental groups, John D. spent more money on saving trees than anyone in the county. He built sub-divisions detouring around trees and moved one they could not skirt. The Norfolk Pine pictured was 65' high when transplanted.*

One of the concerns Palm Beach Shores had was the national attention the town received when the popular audience participation TV show "Treasure Island" was televised from an illegal artificial lake MacArthur dug behind the Colonnades Hotel. The show featured John Bartholomew Tucker, a well known personality as Master of Ceremonies. Contestants had to go by raft to an island in the middle of the lagoon and search for clues that would lead them to the "treasure."

Although the Town Fathers were fighting MacArthur in court at the time, the townsfolk filled the bleachers every day and cheered, hoping for the chance to be seen on coast to coast TV. The show certainly did not hurt the tourist trade for the town's motels and hotel.

In June of 1968 MacArthur brought the College Queen Beauty Contest to Palm Beach

County with the contestants staying at the Colonnades. This contest was also covered on national TV.

Mr. Mac really had a love of trees. On many occasions he insisted that a road be curved in order to save an established grove. Literally hundreds of trees were moved at large expense because MacArthur would not allow them to be mowed down. It was claimed that a world record was made when one of the largest trees, a Banyan was moved and saved. An example of his tree saving legacy can be seen at the corner of North Lake Blvd. and MacArthur Blvd. opposite Costco. A transplanted hundred year old Banyan stands as a living memorial.

By 1968, with the hotel completed and celebrities like Bob Hope coming to town and staying at the Colonnades Hotel, feelings softened and before long Mr. Mac was dressed as Santa Clause and greeting children at the annual Palm Beach Shores Christmas Party. The president of the association even presented the former town's nemesis with an honorary lifetime membership.

North Palm Beach Council deliberated too long when Mr. Mac wanted to have the northern end of Singer Island retained as a nature preserve, so he announced publicly that he was going to develop the land and pave over everything. The land issue was settled immediately and today can be enjoyed as one of the very few and finest original Florida shorelines in the State Park named, as it should be, the John D. MacArthur State Park.

Most millionaires obtained their business degree before being successful. Mr. MacArthur had only a grade school education while accumulating his millions, but in 1976 he received an Honorary Doctorate of Business Administration from Chicago State University. The Advertising Club of the Palm Beaches also awarded the Public Relations Through Public Service Award for his contributions to the development of Palm Beach County and surrounding area in 1969.

The Biltmore Hotel opened in Palm Beach in 1926 as the Alba Hotel in honor of the Duke of Alba, a polo playing buddy of the owner/developer. The cost was over seven million dollars. The "Hard Luck Hotel" would have been a better name. The opening gala was to feature the Duke but he was unable to attend. In order to not disappoint the high society guests, an actor was hired to stand in for him. Unfortunately, the actor was exposed after imbibing a little more than he should have. Even so, the press wrote "Palm Beach's newest hostelry, the Alba, is Palm Beach's greatest monument to those who love the Florida coast and follow the sun. New hotels will rise, but will they rival the rich magnificence of the Alba?"

Within a matter of weeks the hotel was in bankruptcy. It opened the next year as the

Ambassador. That ownership also ended in financial trouble and it was not until many owners later that it hit its peak. By this time it was widely known as the Biltmore. Sadly, the once famous Biltmore, whose guests had included Babe Ruth, General MacArthur, Mary Pickford, and dozens more internationally known celebrities, closed its doors in 1970. John D bought it from the Teamster's Union Pension Fund that had paid $1.5 million at an auction on the courthouse steps. Whether the town thought MacArthur might bring problems to Palm Beach like he had to Palm Beach Shores is not known. What is known is they refused him permission to reopen the Biltmore. He had ample opportunities to sell at a good price, but he insisted that the hotel not be torn down, which all the experts said was the only course of action that made any sense.

The hotel sat empty and in a poor state of repair for years with all of the usual grumbling from the locals. Finally, despite all of the high priced advice, Mr. MacArthur gutted the building, rebuilt it, and sold the individual units as condos. They were the first in the area to demand a million dollar price tag. They were also the only ones to advertise docking space for 200-foot-long yachts. MacArthur's Luck came through one more time.

Mr. Mac seemed to be ahead of his time in his thinking and that may have played a big part in his success. In 1970 he championed the cause of the north county needing adequate housing for all citizens and pushed for modular inexpensive homes. His statements fell on deaf ears and yet 30-plus years later action committees are working on the same problem that now threatens to interfere with the area's prosperity, due to a lack of housing for the local workforce.

According to Mr. Mac, he and his wife of more than 50 years, Catherine, formed the MacArthur Foundation to keep the government from getting their hard earned money. Whatever the reason, all of their riches, including thousand of acres of prime Martin and Palm Beach County land, was placed in a not-for-profit trust. This trust, one of the nation's largest, to this day is financing scholarships and large scale philanthropic programs, to the tune of $100 million a year, with little fanfare.

John D. MacArthur died in January 1978. His best obituary was perhaps a line by local newspaper columnist Steve Mitchell after reminiscing about MacArthur's taste, manners, language and shenanigans. Mitchell wrote, "That was John D, self satisfied, a phenomenon, a character, an original." We could add, "and a very significant chapter of the history of Palm Beach Shores."

# People

In addition to Mr. Singer, Mr. Edwards and Mr. MacArthur, many others have helped to mold Palm Beach Shores into the "Best Little Town in Florida." The danger of trying to recognize all those who have contributed to the development of Palm Beach Shores is the inevitable certainty of overlooking some deserving individual who should be on the list. Still, it is necessary to formulate such a listing with apologies in advance for anyone who might inadvertently go unnoticed.

**Ryder Steen.** Acknowledged as the first business operator, "Steen's Restaurant," on Singer Island and one of the first residents in town.

**Henry Peerson.** First elected mayor of the town and active in all of the early activities.

**Ernest Able.** Long-time Town Clerk as well as Treasurer, Superintendent of Public Works, Tax Assessor and Tax Collector..

**Edgar Bauer.** Edgar, along with his sidekick Mel Schrieber, operated a gift store on Blue Heron Blvd for decades. They closed in the summer and traveled worldwide to find interesting sales items. Both were active in town affairs and Edgar was an Environmental Committee charter member and chairman for many years.

**Bill Bachstet.** Investor / builder who for twenty years owned Bill's Marina, which later became part of Sailfish Marina complex.

**Ed Roerich.** Early town home and apartment builder, thirty plus year resident, partner with Bill Bachstet in Bill's Marina.

**Ruth Douglass.** Convinced Seasiders to sponsor Nativity Scene in 1958. Made and clothed figures from inception through early 1980s.

**Paul Potter.** One of the most active mayors. His four-year tenure was highlighted with many major accomplishments.

**Russell Whetstone.** Fire Chief for 9 early years was responsible for the training and equipment purchases that made the department a capable firefighting force.

**Norris Norman.** Planning and Zoning Board and Town Commission member. Voted for height limitation although it meant lower property value for his Buccaneer Lounge property.

*Midge McNearny honored by Property Owners with the Outstanding Citizen Award.*

**Millie Male.** First woman commissioner. Very active in all town organizations.

**Marty Kastner.** Fire Chief on two occasions. Very active in Property Owners social functions and, along with wife Kay and Ken Frey, pretty much ran the Spring Fling and Christmas Party Dinner time after time.

**Paul and Miriam Klang.** Only husband and wife to serve as mayor. Paul from 1975-1980 and Miriam from 1986-1988.

**Anita Redding.** Along with her committee, authored the original town history booklet written to celebrate the country's bicentennial year.

**The Ernst Family.** Bill Sr. was long-time volunteer fire fighter serving as fireman, Assistant Chief, and Traffic Control Captain. Wife Marie, elected as Town Commissioner and active in Fire Department Women's Auxiliary. Son Bill Jr. was volunteer fireman and daughter Barbara was very active in Women's Auxiliary. She married a Volunteer Fire Department member Bill Cahill.

**Bob Crosby.** Self taught engineer and probably the most detailed building inspector the town ever had. Also served as Town Manager.

**Barbara Weigel.** Served as Town Deputy Clerk, Town Clerk and Town Manager. Service to town spanned time frame of three different mayors.

**Bob Widmann.** Town Commissioner for many years. Was Chief Deputy Sheriff under three different Sheriffs and instituted a program for the Police Department that brought the department up to a competitive level with other agencies.

**Allan Everard.** Served as a prosecutor, defense attorney and Circuit Court Judge before becoming the Palm Beach Shores Attorney in 1970's -80's. Originated many ideas and legal plans that contributed to the town's progress. His favorite question was, "What is it you want to accomplish?"

**Ray Lawrence.** Active town resident. Sat on Planning and Zoning Board, Code Enforcement Board and drew new town zoning map with the help of Bill Kellner.

**Hank Viswat.** Along with his wife, Marge, took pride in keeping the parkway looking good for more than twenty years.

**Bruce Witherspoon.** For twenty years starting in 1979, Bruce welcomed residents by their first name to his Sailfish Marina Galley Restaurant. He invented the Grouper Dog (and owns the copyright name), which is still a big seller at the Marina's Thursday Night Sunset Celebration.

**Sandra Holmes.** Longest serving Deputy Town Clerk and Town Clerk with 17 years service. Only non-police employee to date to retire under town's retirement plan.

**Hank (Hector) Gardner.** Hank was a commissioner, Vice Mayor and chairman of numerous committees. No matter what the task, Hank was willing to do whatever it took to get the job done, from borrowing a rake and jerry-fitting it to the town's tractor, then driving the tractor to rake the beach at daybreak, to heading up the first "Fun Fest" celebration in the Parkway.

**Barbara Sanderson.** Active participant with every group in town. Served on Planning and Zoning Board. Her life was devoted to the town for thirty years.

**Tom Chilcote.** Served as Mayor for 12 years as well as being very active on the Environmental Committee and member of the Top of the Hill Gang.

**George Sylvester.** Headed up the "Fun Fest" for many years. Took on Parking Committee chairmanship as well as Sidewalk and Road Study Committee head.

**Howard Watts.** In 1981 put together crew to conducted early morning turtle patrols along beach. Served as volunteer fireman. Wife Cynthia was Town Commissioner.

**Joe Baccari.** Joe was active in the Fire Department using his experience as an automobile mechanic. Police cars, public works truck and even the fire engine were repaired. Joe also served as a commissioner for many years.

**Nell Ball.** Active seasider, Four Arts trip organizer and for many years headed up the monthly beach cleaning.

**Jim Collins.** (Mr. Research). For many years Jim has taken active part in getting facts to policy makers. State, county and local laws are his bag. He also racks up more mileage in the Citizens On Patrol car than any other C.O.P. member.

**Bill Hayes.** Bill brought calm decisive mannerism to a sometimes raucous commission meeting. He served as a commissioner and Vice Mayor for five years. He headed up important committees, including one that challenged the Seafarer Pipeline Project.

**Barbara Kissas.** For more than nineteen years has been a member of the motorized turtle patrol. She is the head permit holder and certified by the state to handle the endangered sea turtles.

**Pat Maloney.** An active woman who participated in all town activities. Headed committee that rewrote town history booklet.

**Carol Pirro.** Known for her community fund raising successes including Pancake Breakfasts and House Tours.

**Chuck Platner.** Along with wife, Barbara, could easily be described as "Mr. & Mrs. Environmental Committee."

**Larry Fauci.** Present Chief of the Volunteer Fire Department has held this job for 11 years.

**Roger Wille.** Rose through the ranks from patrolman to Chief. Longest serving employee in town's history. Thirty years and still counting.

**Steve Kniffen.** Long term police officer with present rank of Captain. As Administrative Officer he has satisfied numerous commissions with detailed reports and budget preparation.

**Steve Langevin.** Present rank of Lieutenant. Takes credit for formation and management of Community Policing Program, which includes Citizens on Patrol (C.O.P.), Mayor's Youth Council, Crime Watch and citizens monthly meetings.

**Trela White.** Town Attorney for more than fifteen years. Her municipal experience along with her representation of the Palm Beach County Chapter of the Florida League of Cities gives Palm Beach Shores a strong legal position.

**Carolyn Gangwer.** Town Clerk, who handled all the paperwork for development projects while taking care of regular duties, through the town's boom period, 2003 – 2006.

**Cynthia Lindscoog.** Town Administrator managed largest infrastructures improvement in town's history — street lighting, crosswalks, sidewalks, traffic circle, parks, town hall improvements, new community center. All brought in below budget. Obtained 3/4 million dollars in grants for town.

**Karen Marcus.** County Commissioner who came to the town's rescue when it was short of money to complete a long needed sidewalk. She has since helped with numerous projects and is in the town's "Best Friend" category.

**Jeff Atwater.** State Senator Atwater even wears the town logo T-shirt at political functions. Helping to push a bill through the state legislature authorizing 1,200 feet off-shore police jurisdiction to protect the town's beaches also places him in the town's "Best Friend" category.

# Police

Mr. Edwards used part-time employees to act as security while the new subdivision of Palm Beach Shores was under development during the first year of its incorporation. By 1952 the town's growth prompted a need for police presence and in April Richard Trexler and E.A. Ponce were hired as the town's first police officers, one for day shift and one for night. Their contract included performing other miscellaneous duties as directed by the mayor and for this they were paid $250 per month. At the same time, the purchase of a police vehicle was also authorized at a cost of $1,859.

The force expanded in February of 1956 with the addition of one more officer. Mr. Richard Trexler, the town's first policeman, was promoted to Sergeant and is mentioned as the Town Hall desk man in general and the Police Clerk in particular. He later requested a reduction in salary to offset his no cost living in an apartment above Town Hall. Mr. Trexler became the Custodian of Town Buildings when the new position was created in 1960. Paul de Luisa served as Chief with Harold Anderson and Andrew Ribar as patrolmen. The hiring of an additional part-time officer by mid 1957 allowed round the clock one-man patrols of 8 hours each. Patrolman Albert Wolff was appointed Chief in 1958 and started an 18-year career in that position.

During this period the town and the department grew slowly. By 1981 the department consisted of 8 sworn officers and a daytime clerk. A non-growth period of more than 15 years resulted in the force improving as far as acquiring new equipment, but without a necessity for additional personnel. Then came the planning of the Marriott complex. It was determined that the projected number of additional people in town would require a minimum of two officers be on duty round the clock. A program was initiated that would add men as the different buildings were completed. In 2001 an additional officer was added, in 2003 the 10th was hired and in 2005 the 11th officer joined the roster. This compliment of men, along with backup part-time officers, guarantees a minimum of two officers on duty 24 hours a day.

*1957 Policemen. By this time the Palm Beach Shores Police Department had two vehicles, five sworn officers and provided 'round the clock patrols.*

*With the "take home auto program" each sworn officer is responsible for his own patrol vehicle. During emergencies all eleven officers could be on duty with their marked units patrolling along with the C.O.P. car providing a very visable presense.*

The force is served by a highly trained staff of professional dispatchers, qualified in 911 emergency procedures. The system itself is known as an "enhanced 911 system," which automatically determines the address of the caller. The system is the same one that is found in large cities and Palm Beach Shores is one of the very few small communities to enjoy such an installation. The net result is the police can respond to any call within 2 minutes to any location in town, 24/7. With the newly initiated take-home auto program, where each officer has a vehicle assigned to him personally, a shift change can look like a police convention. At these times it is hard to believe that there are only eleven fulltime sworn officers. During the hurricanes of 2004 and 2005, curfews were initiated and patrols doubled. Police vehicles were on every street to give residents a comforting sense of security.

Serving a small town is not every police officer's forte, but based on the longevity of some who have served, the ones who fit in seem to like it. Chief Wolff set the standard with his 18-year service. Retired Lt. Lou Soldo served for 24 years  As of the beginning of 2006 Chief Roger Wille has over 30 years with the department, Captain Steve Kniffin a little more than 25 years, and Lieutenant Steve Langevin so far has served 12 years. Only four men have held the position of Chief in the town's 54-year history, a claim that not many communities can make.

The police originally operated out of a small office in Town Hall. This was adequate with only one officer on duty, but by the 1960s more space was needed. When the fire hall was built in 1965, the rear portion was dedicated as the new police station. By 1980 the department was once again busting at the seams and a separate addition, at a cost of $18,000 was completed in 1981. This station served until 2003 when the building housing the pumps, generators and motors for the town's water supply was converted. This building is the second oldest building in town. It was refurbished as the Police Annex, giving the senior officers adequate office space in addition to kitchen and shower facilities for times when double shifts were needed as well as an enlarged evidence room.

The equipment issued to officers has come a long way, as shown by the comparison of inventories over the years. In 1960 the list showed: 1 Jap Binoculars; 1 Beach Torpedo Buoy; 1 Night Stick; 1- 5 Cell Flashlight; 1 Sun Helmut; 1- 8-inch Slapper; 2- 6-inch Slapper (listed as Slapper, but also known as a sap or sapper). Officers now have direct communications with state and county agencies, computers for internet training and report writing, thermal imaging guns that can locate a person by detecting the heat given off by his body, and night vision equipment to give officers eyes in the dark. Each officer has his own police automobile equipped with all the necessary tools from an AED (Automatic Emergency Defibrillator) to a finger print lifting kit.

With the additional personnel it has been possible to initiate a regular bicycle patrol as well as a marine unit to patrol the borders of the town from the lake, inlet and ocean.

The crime rate is extremely low in Palm Beach Shores, a town that seldom makes the evening news. Here's a potpourri of some of the town's newsworthy historical incidents:

On Friday May 11, 1973, Officer Ken Fisher completed his twelve hour shift, collected his pay check and hopped into his bright green dune buggy. He proceeded to the bank at what was the Twin City Mall at the corner of U.S. 1 and North Lake Boulevard. As he approached the bank he heard a woman scream and then saw a teenager, later identified as a runaway from Baltimore, holding the woman at gun point. When the robber saw Patrolman Fisher he started to run, but stopped three different times to turn and fire at Fisher. He also took one shot at another bystander. After the third shot Fisher took aim and from about 200 feet shot the fleeing robber in the shoulder. Even after being shot the perpetrator continued to run out onto U.S. 1 where a school bus full of elementary school children was stuck in traffic. He entered and commandeered the bus from the front entrance while seven kids escaped through the rear emergency exit. The rest began a frightful odyssey down the highway to Blue Heron Boulevard. Meanwhile Officer Fisher returned to his dune buggy and followed the bus at a safe distance. A road block finally stopped the bus at the Blue Heron Bridge and Lakeshore Drive. Fourteen-year-old John Lemasters was arrested. Patrolman Kenneth Fisher was a local hero and his bright green dune buggy was recognized wherever he traveled in the north county for quite some time.

In September of 1973, fifteen year department veteran Lt. Lee Williams answered a call at the Colonnades regarding a guest having a disagreement with the hotel's staff. The on duty manager wanted the guest to leave immediately, The guest agreed to leave, but only after reimbursement for the package deal he had prepaid. Lt. Williams agreed with the guest. At the next Property Owners' meeting, John D MacArthur, the town's billionaire and owner of the Colonnades Hotel, showed up and claimed that, although he was not personally present at the time of the incident, he had it on good authority that Lt. Williams was abusive and drunk when he answered the call. A review by the police chief and the mayor could not substantiate the charges and the commission voted not to take any action, but the police officer found himself in an "untenable" position and resigned his commission. The entire incident was captured in all the local news media. He left the force in March of 1974.

On February 13, 1976 Patrolman Roger Wille was conducting a standard security check at the Buccaneer Yacht Club when he encountered three juveniles ransacking the office. He managed to arrest one of the suspects and called Chief Roberson for backup, who immediately responded from his home. As they investigated the scene they discovered a fire which filled a room with smoke and an unconscious man inside. Chief Roberson pulled the victim to safety. All three juveniles were later arrested and their arrest cleared three other non-residential and one residential burglaries. All of the stolen loot was recovered and returned to the rightful owners.

In October of 1976, a 37-foot sport fishing vessel arrived at Cannonsport Marina for an overnight stay. During the closing time dock check, the dock attendant noticed the boat sitting low in the water. The crew had already departed so he went onboard to check the lazzarette bilge for signs of the vessel taking on water. When he lifted the hatch he could not see the bilge. The compartment was full of burlap bags of marijuana. He reported the find to the owner, who in turn called the Coast Guard and reported a sinking boat. Before long the dock was swarming with Coast Guard personnel, Palm Beach Shores Police and Palm

*The town beach is protected with a life guard seven days a week. The highly qualified unit is a subsidary of the Police Department as is the 911 Dispatch.*

Beach County Sheriff Deputies. Four thousand pounds of drugs worth $1.25 million was confiscated. Palm Beach Shores Police were given the job of unloading the boat and guarding the 60-odd bags overnight. The next day state prisoners were brought in to remove and burn the stash. (Reports of funny behavior of the cows in the downwind pastures were not confirmed.) The boat was of little value, but it was forfeited and sold at public auction. The money was used to buy a new copy machine for Town Hall.

In May of 1977 a beautiful blonde German girl stayed at the Colonnades Hotel. She was apparently working her way around the globe in the world's oldest profession. A guest of the hotel had made use of her favors and afterwards discovered his watch missing. He left the room and called the police. Chief Robby Roberson took off his uniform shirt, put on a plain one and was introduced to the Fräulein as a friend of the original client. He was immediately propositioned. The blonde's globe-trotting plans ended abruptly with a visit to the station's holding cell. By all accounts she was one of the cells more attractive visitors.

The most infamous visitor to town was without a doubt underworld figure Joseph Iannuzzi, nicknamed "Joe Dogs" due to his penchant for gambling at greyhound races. In the late summer of 1980, patrolling police officers found a nude victim of a severe beating in the grass near the edge of the roadway on Cascade Lane. The male victim was close to death and only the immediate care administered by the officers and a fast trip to the hospital saved his life. A preliminary investigation revealed that Joe Dogs was involved and they were dealing with an attempted homicide.

Chief Roger Wille asked for the assistance of the Palm Beach County Sheriff who assigned Detective Ed Bieulich to the case. The homicide investigation determined that Joey had caught his girlfriend in bed with the victim and had ordered two of his henchmen to get rid of him by pistol whipping. They had not expected that he would live, let alone be able to crawl outside and be found.

Joey's favorite hangout was the Top o' the Spray Lounge. After a brief stakeout, Chief Wille, Officer Bob Radcliffe and Detective Bieulich, who would later be elected Palm Beach County's Sheriff, apprehended Joey and charged him with attempted homicide. He bonded out of jail and was right back in town almost immediately, this time renting a complete floor of the Colonnades Hotel and setting up shop in the lounge. It was not exactly the type of public relations the town was looking for. Chief Wille called in help from other law enforcement agencies and they conducted an open and legal harassment, which caused Joe Dogs to corner the Chief after a few days and ask, "What will it take to get you off my ass?" The Chief replied the problem would go away if Joey would relocate to the other side of the town entry sign. Joey and his entourage were gone the next day.

Joey again made local news in January of 1981 when he received a mob beating from members of the Gambino family. It seems that Joe Dogs had missed a payment on a loan he received from "Tommy A" Agro, a reputed soldier in the Gambino mob. Agro traveled to Florida with two of his henchmen to pay Joey a visit and remind him of his obligation. The baseball bat reminder took place in a pizza parlor on the island in Riviera Beach. His injuries were not life threatening only because the wife of the owner entered the kitchen and began screaming.

Four years later the FBI revealed that Joey had, for a long period of time, been working as an informer for them in an attempt to get at some higher ups in the Gambino family. When Joey was told by his bosses in New York to clear the way for a new gambling club in the area, the FBI gave their blessing and assigned a Chicago agent to be his partner. The project was called "Operation Home Run" and the Beach Side Nightclub on Singer Island opened. The Chicago agent was not only accepted by the mob but actually made "Capo" in the Gambino family. The operation photographed, videotaped and recorded suspects and snared more than a dozen mobsters. Corrupt local officials were also targeted including Riviera Police Chief Boone Darden.

Later in 1981 Joe Dogs, wired for sound, met with Boone and recorded a conversation that lead to Darden's indictment for accepting payoffs from organized crime figures and his eventual sentence to prison.

Besides the incriminating evidence of corrupt action, the tape also contained a casual compliment to the Palm Beach Shores Police. The following conversation transpired when Iannuzzi complained to Darden that (Chief) Roger Wille had banned him from Palm Beach Shores:

"Yeah, don't want me in that town," Iannuzzi said laughing.

Darden asked, "He said that to your face?"

"Yeah, he don't want me in Palm Beach Shores. That's why I don't go to the Colonnades no more."

In September 2002 Palm Beach Shores Police were the first on scene when a woman suffered a heart attack. Officer Vincent Walasek determined that no pulse existed, applied CPR and then hooked up a newly purchased AED (defibrillator). After numerous tries the woman began to breathe. Three months later Vince received a citation for his lifesaving act, but the biggest reward was receiving a kiss from the, by then, fully recuperated lady, who attended the ceremony.

In 2004 and 2005 the town was hit with the most powerful hurricanes in its history. Authority to run the town under these circumstances is turned over by the mayor to the Emergency Manager, who has always been the Police Chief. The force is divided into two groups with one group staying in town during the hurricane and one coming back immediately after the storm passes. Hurricane Frances, the first of the three storms, took so long to pass through and did such major destruction in the general area that the original team did not leave until 58 continuous hours after they reported for duty. This group was under the command of Captain Steve Kniffin who documented all the storms in diary fashion, starting when the first warning was received and continuing until things were back to normal. These journals, complete with photos, will be the historical information for future generations.

During Hurricane Wilma in 2005, another heart attack 911 call came into dispatch from Inlet Way. The caller(s) was performing CPR on the victim. Unfortunately, the winds at this time were at 80 miles per hour, well above the minimum of 40 mph that dictates fire rescue team operations. Police officers made the decision to answer the call even though they had a perfect reason to play it safe and stay indoors. Two officers responded along with a fire department volunteer who was an EMT. They stabilized the patient then brought him to the safety of the police station, where they made him comfortable and monitored him until the storm had passed. Fire Rescue then arrived and transported him to the hospital. The men who answered the call were Lt. Steve Langevin, Officer Tom Clark and Firefighter Richard Salmon. All three were awarded lifesaving medals based on the fact they put their own life in jeopardy when answering the call.

The change from what was typically little, if any, formal training policing to the entrance into a modern proactive force started in 1975 when the first chief with professional training and experience was hired. Chief Roberson held senior positions with both the Palm Beach Police Department and the Palm Beach Gardens Police Department before coming to the little town of Palm Beach Shores. He immediately recruited a sergeant with whom he had worked in the Gardens, Roger Wille, and later Lou Soldo from the Palm Beach force. He introduced standardized procedures, reports and record keeping. New young officers, most with some previous training either with other departments or in the military, soon formed the force's nucleus. The progression has been maintained in such a way that the department operates under a standard that many large cities have not attained. State Accreditation is reserved only for communities that are willing to commit to the time and expense that allows them to meet a level of professionalism that must be maintained with periodic testing and inspections. The policies and procedures are the same as those followed by the largest cities and counties. Palm Beach Shores proudly holds that accreditation.

The Palm Beach Shores Police Department has come a long way from the days when the officer on duty brought his fishing pole to work with him. Today the town is protected with highly trained personnel using the most modern equipment in a highly structured paramilitary setting. Such a police department is rare in small towns.

*Officers in attendance at September 11, 2002 memorial service. Also attending but not in picture was the Chief, Captain and Lieutenant.*

*As well as protecting the town, the Chief found time to pose with these Riviera Beach Chamber of Commerce Beauty Contest Contestants.*

# Fire

During the first decade of the town's existence, Palm Beach Shores enjoyed fire protection by contracting with the City of Riviera Beach. When the city, in 1963, demanded a new fire protection contract costing the town *one mill of assessed valuation and only promising service on an "if available basis,"* the mayor and commission balked. The only station in Riviera at the time was on the mainland and the bridge to the island was a drawbridge. Delays were not unusual on the single lane road during the season and when the bridge was open for boating traffic, serious delays would occur at any time of the year. The decision was made to investigate the feasibility of other means of fire protection. When subsequent negotiations failed to produce an acceptable compromise, the Town Commission determined that the best course of action was for the town to provide its own protection by organizing and equipping a volunteer fire department.

The planning came to fruition on October 30, 1963 when an organizational meeting was held, officers were elected and articles of incorporation were signed, establishing the Palm Beach Shores Fire Department Inc. The corporation was chartered "to preserve and protect the lives and property of the residents of Palm Beach Shores." Thirty eight members signed up with 30 of these eligible for unlimited fire fighting service. The men were divided in sections by age and whether they were in town during the day or just at night or both. Eight were assigned to be on 24-hour call, fifteen for day time and seven for nights only. In July of 1964 eighteen members completed training presented by the State Fire College. Many are still town residents today, such as Gerald Schumm, Donald Sirl and John Cheraso. The youngest firefighter was Guy Hill. Guy grew up in town and then raised his family here. He was later honored with a lifetime honorary membership. Within a year most of the volunteers, including the commissioners led by Mayor Paul Potter had received similar training and adequate fire fighting equipment was purchased with an indebtedness of one half mil over a four-year term. Equipment life was

*Palm Beach Shores Volunteers take a break during mutual assistance call to help North Palm Beach firemen battle a fire that caused over a million dollar in damages at the Old Port Cove complex."*

determined to be twenty years. So for one half the cost requested by Riviera Beach and with indebtedness of only four years, instead of "forever," the town would have full availability of fire fighting resources, not just "if available." As a bonus, fire fighting response time would not be controlled by boat traffic in the Intracoastal Waterway. On January 1964 the town received bids for a 500-gallon fire engine on a Ford chassis. Although the first resolution to the association's articles of incorporation stated that the association would endeavor to be financially self-sustaining from the start, the town has always supplied the equipment for the department. The funds raised by the volunteers in the early days were used to help purchase budgeted items, thereby saving the town funds. As the tax base grew. the town picked up 100% of necessary equipment with fundraiser monies spent on ancillary items. In 1978 a second engine was added. This one was a Mack pumper painted the "new" yellow-lime color. The firehouse was enlarged in 2004 to accommodate the newest addition to the fleet, a Pierce Contender enclosed cab unit painted a conventional red and white. The department continued to grow each year with more modern equipment as well as better training of its personnel.

One of the first major fire calls the new department received was a call for mutual assistance from the Riviera Beach F.D. During the riots in the summer of 1967, in the west end of the city, rioters had set fire to the Mullen's Lumber Yard. volunteers were welcomed with their brand new engine and performed back-up duties throughout the night led by then Mayor Paul Potter.

In the 1980's a shortage of volunteers prompted the combining of the Fire and Police Department to form a Public Safety Unit. Only two volunteers had the state minimum training of 40 hours. Although this unit was short lived, three police officers, including Chief Wille, attended and graduated from the State Fire College and in so doing became the town's first fully certified firefighters.

The town has been fortunate in finding a qualified Fire Chief to run the department since the beginning. For many years the chief was the only compensated member of the department as an employee of the town. A part-time Fire Inspector was later added and in recent years eligible firefighters have been paid both a bonus and a small compensation based on their training and firefighting participation.

The first Fire Chief was Walter Scheff who helped organize and get the department up and running from October of 1963 through June of 1964. He was followed by Chief Frank Henry who served until Chief Russell Whetstone took over in February of 1965. Whetstone was a Colonel in the U.S. Army and brought with him a para-military system of operation. Col.

*P.B.S.V.F.D. 'Miss Flame' Beauty Contest Winner, 1965."*

*Police and Firemen attended the 2002 anniversary ceremony for the 9/11/01 terroist attack of the N.Y. Twin Towers.*

Whetstone served for nine years and is given the credit for putting in place many of the routines and reports that are still followed today.

Marty Kastner was Fire Chief on two occasions, from 1974 to 1976 and again from 1993 through 1995. Al Holmes is one of two chiefs who served as leader the longest, with a span of 11 years starting in 1976. Most of the chiefs have been retirees with previous firefighting experience, but not so with John Gosline. John was the town's youngest chief at 22 years of age. His forte was his expertise in fluid dynamics and commercial automatic sprinkler systems. Larry Joyce would be rated the tallest (6' 8") and most jovial while putting in his time between 1986 and 1992. The current Fire Chief, Larry Fauci, also has 11 years of service, having served since 1995, and is expected to set a new longevity record.

The chief, while only paid for a twenty-hour week, actually puts in many extra hours and is responsible for the readiness of the equipment, the continual training of the men, and all of the attendant paperwork. (Chief Fauci, over a five-year period logged an average of 422 extra hours per year). By charter he reports directly to the mayor.

In the last few years every multifamily building and each home with a home office license is inspected on a regular basis by the Fire Inspector. The town's safety record is extremely good, thanks to the many fire prevention programs, the inspections, and the quick response of the firefighters when a problem does occur.

Although the safety record is great, major fires have occurred. In 1978 a fire at the Sailfish Marina engulfed three large yachts. The ensuing inferno had all the elements of a movie—excitement, chaos, bravery, leadership and comedy. Firefighter Hank Gardner, while handling a charged fire hose stepped backward off the dock into 20 feet of water, wearing full firefighting gear. It was a very serious incident when it happened, but Hank was the butt of jokes for years. Cannonsport Marina was not to be left out. The very next season a sixty foot motor vessel burned almost to the waterline taking out a portion of the marina's fuel dock. Luckily the wind, although strong, was blowing the flames away from the other boats and they were all moved to safety. A year later the Buccaneer Marina had a fire that could have been disastrous. However, the quick response of the department allowed firefighters to contain the blaze to one boat. There is a secondary major problem in fighting boat fires the conventional way. By using high volumes of water to extinguish the flames, the boat is very likely to sink unless a pump can be installed early in the firefighting episode. This was a problem at all of the boat fires experienced.

*1964 Certificates of Basic Firefighting Course earned by the original Volunteers.*

The Colonnades, being the largest building in town for many years, was a major concern to the Fire Department. Three fires are worthy of mention. Colonnades owner John D. MacArthur made the news when a cigarette caused a sofa to smolder, filling his apartment and adjoining hallway with smoke. Mr. MacArthur described his role in a heroic manner, relating how he crawled through the smoke on hands and knees, directing the firemen to the apartment door. Chief Kastner was very diplomatic in his press interview. He, in a very polite manner, said that the biggest problem in putting out the fire was working around, and finally having to take care of, Mr. MacArthur.

A more serious fire engulfed a street front room of the hotel and had the possibility of spreading in all directions. Larry Joyce, who was a Captain in the North Palm Beach Public Safety organization (later Chief of Palm Beach Shores Volunteers), was coming over the bridge onto the island when he saw flames from the Colonnades Hotel. He went directly to the fire and observed the town's firemen aiming the engine mounted deluge gun up at the sliding glass doors of the third floor room on fire. He proceeded to take a 1 1/2" line up the three flights of inside stairs and fought the fire from the hallway corridor. There was a look of surprise on the faces of the crew on the street when Joyce stepped out onto the balcony and yelled down to them, "Get your ass up here!"

The third incident occurred in November of 1980 when an alarm sounded that would get the adrenalin levels peaking in any firefighter.

*1965 Volunteers during training session with State Fire College teacher( in checkered shirt.)*

The seven story south building of the Colonnades was on fire. Smoke completely filled the Ballroom and was exiting the building from various locations. Following is a copy of the Officer in Charge's report outlining the procedures of the Volunteer Fire Department. The report is written after the fire is out when it is easy to cite the rules of encounter. Waking from a deep sleep at 4:00 in the morning and putting it all together under the fire scene circumstances would definitely not be quite as precise or matter of fact as the report reads.

*Colonnades South building is a seven story structure. Only ten rooms were occupied in the early morning of November 24, 1980.*

*Southernmost side of building has a one (1) story concrete supported area running the full depth of the building. The structure is of wood beam, drywall and plywood construction with a tar/gravel roof. This area houses Maintenance, Linen, Laundry, Ball Room Kitchen, Wash Rooms, Storage Room and Tennis Pro Shop. (Listed, road to ocean sequence) The area is not serviced by sprinkler system.*

*Police Officer Mitch Woodruff answered call placed at 04:10 a.m. by a Nancy Siegel of Malibo Apts. Reporting smoke in area. At 04:12 a.m. Officer Woodruff confirmed call and requested fire alarm through Sheriff's office.*

*Upon arrival at the station, I ascertained that Engine 81 was ready to roll with eight (8) men (including myself). I ordered two (2) men to wait with Engine 82 and proceeded to site after insuring that a driver for Engine 82 was available.*

*Arrived on scene at approximately 04:17 a.m. and observed major area of dense smoke including all of Ballroom, Lobby and second and third floor balconies. Fire location was not immediately apparent. Requested mutual aid from Riviera Beach Fire Department. Police and hotel management cleared the (ten) 10 occupied rooms. Two, two-men teams sent to locate source of fire. Team sent to south side of building located fire in Linen / Laundry area. Approximately 60' x 30' was ablaze, two sets of double doors twenty feet apart were locked but flames could be seen through door centers. After positioning booster at one door and the 1 1/2" hose at the other, the doors were broken open and fire fighting proceeded. Determined that fire could be successfully fought with the available crews and cancelled mutual aid request. Engine 82 arrived and 3" supply line was run and in operation before 81 ran dry. Approximately 40 minutes with 3 nozzles were required to extinguish blaze.*

*The damage to the immediate area was severe (gutted) with hotel management* *estimate of $5,000 structural damage; $5,000 loss of linens and unappraised but extensive smoke damage to bar, ballroom, corridors and guest rooms. Clean up was completed at 06:30 a.m. and Engine 82 released.*

*Engine 81 released at 07:00 a.m., hoses hung, repacked and pumper greased, air packs changed, fire site secured and State Fire Marshal informed. Arrangements made with Palm Beach Gardens F.D. to refill air packs in afternoon. Determined that replacement hose was not required. Crew dismissed at 08:00 a.m. (except for security at hotel). At 10:15 released site to hotel management.*

*Major damage was avoided (fire spreading) due to fact that the area of fire was a one story structure and through timely alarm and response. Fire was spreading towards adjacent ballroom which is part of multistory area of hotel, but fire was contained to service area.*

*Ten (10) Firemen and five (5) Traffic Control Officers answered alarm.*

*Photos were taken by Dick Fenton and George Hironimus.*

*Intensive heat area was adjacent to South outside wall and located high above floor level. Cause of fire not determined and is pending Fire Marshal investigation.*

Most current volunteers are certified as Firefighter I. This requires 160 hours of formal training by instructors from the State Fire College. Some members have the more extensive Firefighter II designation, several are E.M.T. certified, and one has full paramedic credentials.

The volunteers have the most modern equipment available, including cameras that see through smoke, and are backed up by the professional crews from the City of Riviera Beach, North Palm Beach and Palm Beach Gardens if needed. They continue to provide a service few other small towns enjoy.

*A Fire Department tradition. Santa distributes candy to kids from fire engines on Christmas morning.*

# Fire Department Ladies Auxiliary

Almost as well known as the Fire Department itself, the Fire Department's Ladies Auxiliary was formed on October 12, 1977 when the wives of seven firefighters got together in what turned out to be the organizational meeting of the group. As a result of the meeting the Ladies Auxiliary of the Palm Beach Shores Volunteer Fire Department came into existence with the stated purpose of "Helping our Firemen." Marie Ernst was the first President, with Scotti Holmes as Vice President, Evelyn Gardner as Secretary and Julia Baker as the first Treasurer.

Originally only wives of firefighters were allowed to join. The treasury was established with a fifty dollar donation from the Fire Department, but fundraising was an item on the agenda at the first meeting. Ten days later, an inter-department open house was scheduled with the Lake Park Fire Department. The new group agreed to supply sandwiches and other refreshments. A total of twelve members were on the roll by the end of the first month.

Many functions were considered as a public service and for fundraising. Sale of T shirts, dinners, a dance and even a Bingo game were suggested, but the first was a hamburger and hot dog sale at the beach pavilion. After cooking and selling 33 hamburgers and 60 hot dogs along with 50 sodas, a grand total profit of $8.32 was realized!

It was a function first held in 1981 that became the event for which the Auxiliary is best known — the regularly held card party. At first, ladies were invited to play cards and enjoy a dessert and coffee for a two dollar donation. Sandwiches were soon added and before long the party was a luncheon where cards were played. Over the years the venue has included the Mayan Towers II Game Room, the Colonnades Hotel and the Town Hall Meeting Room. The party has become so successful that seating is limited by the size of the room.

The group has raised funds over the years that have been donated to the fire department to purchase ancillary equipment. They are regularly seen dispensing meals at the Firemen's Cookouts, while looking very much a team in their matching fire engine red shirts.

The expertise they have gained in feeding large groups have caused them to be called upon to provide catering when the town hosts special meetings for visiting groups, such as the League of Cities. They participate in the Fire Department's regular steak cookouts and help at all open houses, engine dedications and other Fire Department celebrations. They use some of the funds to throw a "thank you" Christmas party for the volunteers each year.

Although prepared to uphold their stated purpose of "helping our firemen," they have not had much occasion to aid firemen at the fire scene with cold drinks (or hot drinks) and refreshments simply because fires are a rare occurrence in Palm Beach Shores. But when needed, they are ready. In September of 1981 a blaze at the Old Port Cove complex in North Palm Beach caused millions of dollars in damages. Palm Beach Shores Volunteers responded along with four other departments. The fire continued for hours and the ladies showed up and served drinks to all the thirsty firemen on the scene.

Also, a house fire in town and a room fire at the Colonnades once again had the ladies responding.

Whether serving as a welcoming committee for visiting V.I.P.s, providing card game entertainment for residents, or quenching the thirst of firefighters in the line of duty, the Ladies Auxiliary of the Palm Beach Shores Volunteer Fire Department has become a town institution that is one of the prides of Palm Beach Shores.

*Although formed with the purpose of 'helping our firemen' the Ladies Auxiliary is involved with most town activities.*

# Chain Gang

In 1954 some Seasiders (women's social club described on page 54) convinced their husbands to form a voluntary group of physically able men to complete some work in town. The Property Owners Association got on board and the town agreed to finance the material cost of selected projects. One gentleman named Al Bohny is given credit for organizing the group and it was originally called "Bohny's Gang."

The projects undertaken were very significant. First, sidewalks, from the beach parking lot to the lifeguards stand were installed. Then came a concrete block retaining wall to keep the parking lot free from drifting sand, along with showers for the beach goers, and an open air pavilion with a beautiful palm frond roof. Next, a sidewalk from the fountain area all the way to the inlet was constructed.

For two years this devoted group worked weekends and evenings in their labor of love. The group's membership changed over time, but the name remained into the early seventies when it was changed to the "Over the Hill Gang" and later to the "Top of the Hill Gang."

The Gang has supplied thousand of hours for town improvement and maintenance over the years. Not only is the cost savings significant, but, more importantly, volunteerism has become a fiber of the town that is reflected in all other organizations, all thanks to what is now known as the "Chain Gang."

The original members were Al Bohny; Jack Pearson; Joe Fuller; Joseph Wood; Horace Kurtz; Blake Crabill; Mayo Fisk; Bob McBrien; Wheaton Douglass; Jay Pridham; George Dougan; Jay Stephens; Bill Bachstet; Gerry Schulz and Homer Parshall. The wives kept them supplied with sandwiches and cold drinks.

At the turn of this century the tradition continued with names such as Tom Chilcote; Jim Allen; Charlie Ball; Al Black; Jim Dagostino; Irv Dawson; Bill Degnon; Don Emens; Bill Ernst Sr.; Fred Hampf; Hank Viswat; Bob Heslin; Hank Gardner; George Sylvester; Vince Allora and Ray Woloszak some wives and many others.

Although a lack of volunteers has been noticed with the change in the town's demographics, as long as this group of men and women show up for work, the spirit of the Chain Gang will go on.

*Original Chain Gang take time out for a photo during construction of pavilion at town's beach. Note the Palm frond roof.*

# Property Owners Association

While Mr. Edwards still had control of the town, serving as mayor with his two employees as commissioners, the new residents were concerned that their best interest may not have been protected. The Property Owners Association was founded in 1950, although not chartered until 1953, and its original purpose was to challenge Mr. Edwards' operation methods. The plan was to have an elected commission by 1954. The Property Owners wanted the transition sooner. When it was pointed out the cost of running the town was being paid by the development company including security, garbage collection, maintenance, clerical and management payrolls and many others. The owners saw the light and dropped their demands.

An interesting situation did develop after the town gained its independence from the developer and that was due to the fact that the beach and parkways were owned by Mr. Edwards but deeded for the exclusive use of legitimate property owners in the development. The elected officials gave the administration of the beach to a new committee, called the Beach and Parkway Authority. They issued metal tags to owners and the beach was limited to town residents, who owned property. During this period the Property Owners Association was instrumental in designing the rules and regulations for the beach and the parkway. They also supplied the volunteers (the Chain Gang) who built the sand retaining wall and sidewalk at the beach and the sidewalk throughout the parkway. They, on two separate occasions suggested that the beach and parkway be sold to them in an attempt to make these lands closed to non-residents.

Their interaction with the commission was quite formal with long wordy letters from the president to the mayor explaining the association's stand on a particular issue. The commission would discuss the issue and then would give the mayor instructions to answer the request. In one 1960 case the mayor's answer contained 12 points covered in four legal pages. Whereas the reply started in a friendly salutation, "I would commend your organization for the forthright and business like manner of submitting your proposal" the last paragraph was curt. "I feel that the Beach and Parkway Authority and the Property Owners Association have just about all the authority they could ask for at the present time." By June of 1963, the roster showed 166 paid memberships representing 315 individuals.

Over the years the P.O.A. gradually picked up the social events started by the Seasiders. These included the annual Christmas party which has hosted over 300 attendees and the spring dinner dance where 202 people were served, the home lighting contest, and other timely affairs. The spring dinner dance now known as the Spring Fling usually had a dress up theme and over the years has seen Western, The Forties, Gay 90's, Construction, Flappers, Formal, Circus and Roman dress. The evening in Ancient Rome was the town's first Toga party.

They have also been instrumental in leading various causes, both independently and at the request of the Town Commission. Included are the fight to stop the Corps of Engineers from blasting in the channel (1964-65); petitions to four lane the bridge onto the island (1967-74); limiting the scope of a rehab center in town (1998-99); petitioning to keep home rule (2005-06) just to name a few.

A newsletter was started and for decades has kept members up to date with town happenings. The early newsletter had a separate section for the Seasiders and almost a verbatim copy of the commission meetings minutes. Eventually the Seasiders needed more space and when the commission minutes began to be edited, both the Seasiders and the town brought out their own newsletters.

Of the 42 members who held the position of association's presidents, four have served as mayor and six have been commissioners. The organization is still a very strong voice of the people and the "doers" of most social events in town.

*Property Owners Association volunteer work parties were responsible for many of the town's early projects.*

# Seasiders

In January of 1951, three months before Palm Beach Shores became a town, six ladies met at the home of a Mrs. Carr who lived at 201 Sandal Lane. The purpose was to determine if there was an interest to form a women's social club that would allow the ever growing number of newcomers to the development to get to know each other.

All of the women were enthusiastic about the idea and decided that such a club would be strictly social and non-political. A second meeting was held at a Mrs. Keith's home at 26 Lake Drive and most of the original members were elected or appointed as officers: Mrs. Keith as President; Mrs. Carr as General Manager; Mrs. Wheelihan, Recording Secretary; Mrs. Russo, Treasurer; Mrs. Carter, Membership Chairman; and Louise James, Social Chairman. Louise and her husband still live in town and can claim the title of residents living in town the longest.

The first name suggested for the group was the Shores Club, then Mrs. Carter said, "Why not the Seasiders?" The ladies asked, "Why not indeed?" and the group that was to become the most influential organization in the town had a name. The toughest assignment was the Membership Chairman since, with no telephone in the development, contact had to be made in person. The direct route from one of the few homes to another was over sand dunes and scrub.

At this meeting the club's objectives were also adopted "to promote the spirit of service and friendship among its members and to stimulate interest in the community." Meetings were to be held twice a month at the Bahia Mar Yacht Club (Buccaneer), the first Wednesday to be a business meeting and the third Wednesday a social. Membership teas were held and proved to be quite successful.

The club grew rapidly. The first social event was a mid-summer party at the Bahia Mar Yacht Club, the highlight of which was an all male cast wedding skit, written by Louise James. Husbands were roped into performing and the organization got off to a great start with the attendees not only enjoying the show but getting a chance to meet their new neighbors, many for the first time.

By Christmas of 1951, the Seasiders, then 66 members strong, held a Christmas lighting contest and convinced Mrs. Pridham's husband Jay to drive his truck around town full of caroling children. At the March 1952 meeting, Mrs. Carr was elected President for the next year and she was installed along with the other new officers at an April dinner dance held at the Colonnades Ocean Terrace Room.

Outgoing President Mrs. Keith reported her pride in the gardening and beautification projects and the charitable fundraising the club had successfully completed in its first year.

That first year set the standard for the club and it quickly took the lead in putting together year round social functions. The 1953-54 season alone saw a Christmas Dinner Dance, a Christmas Lighting Contest, a January Fashion Show, a Red Cross Fund Drive, (the first organization to exceed their goal on the Florida

*Growth from six ladies in 1951 to this group in 1953 proved the idea of a Women's Club was timely. The Seasiders have been the leaders of all town activities since their founding.*

east coast), a similar drive for Cancer Research, and a Mad Hatters party, as well as their installation dinner with sixty ladies in attendance. Fashion shows and Mad Hatters parties are still occasional Seasiders happenings.

*The annual bazaar is a very popular item and has contributed much of the $76,000 that the Seasiders have donated to local charities.*

Besides the social activities, the Seasiders also were the driving force behind the improvements in the town. Their husbands were enjoined to create, through the Property Owner's Association, a work party, i.e., the Chain Gang, who built the seawall at the public beach as well as the original sidewalk throughout the parkway. The ladies were always on hand to provide refreshments for these weekend work parties.

The 1953 yearbook listed seventy-seven members with two active groups of service, one being the Civic and Welfare and the other the Gardening and Beautification. The first project was to make Johnny shirts and bed pads for County Home residents and to increase membership through membership teas. In April of 1958 members authorized a change in the by-laws that allowed the formation of four groups. The Community Service replaced the Civic and Welfare; the Gardening and Beautification kept its name and the Four Arts and Social Affairs came into being. These groups got off to a fast start with the Four Arts meeting twice a month and the Beautification taking on a major Parkway project. The social group held a dinner dance attended by 133 people, a summer picnic at the beach, the first card party held at Town Hall, a luncheon, including cards and swimming, at the Palm Beach Sailfish Club, a Halloween Party and a Christmas lighting contest.

Originally meeting once a month, the community service group's popularity demanded a more active schedule and for many years have been getting together three times a month, in Town Hall. The ladies bring their own sandwich for lunch and arrange to have coffee and dessert supplied. Town Hall staff looks forward to Thursday morning as they get to share the desserts the ladies bring. Each week it seems the ladies try to outdo each other with bigger and better concoctions.

The baking skills turned out to good advantage when the group held a "Gourmet Sale" of delicacies including cakes, pies, bread, candy and relishes. This fundraiser continued throughout the sixties. In 1965 the community service ladies dressed 50 dolls for the Salvation Army Christmas drive. This became a regular Christmas gift for a few more years. In 1967 they conducted a "Bake and Buy" sale. This sale also had a White Elephant table and was the predecessor of the famous annual Bazaar. The 1973 B&B sale included a second table for "new and used but not abused" items. The Bazaar was held in November up until 1988 as a Christmas sale, but it was eventually moved to February to accommodate those snowbirds who do not visit until after the holidays.

Growth of the Bazaar was helped in novel ways; in 1987 S&H Green Stamps were collected; in 1988 it was a casseroles specials; "anything in a bottle" in 1989; jewelry in 1990; books in 1990; fresh flowers in 2004; and a 50 / 50 drawing in 2005. The book sale caused some confusion when the group advertised for pocket books and received many purses as well as books… English is a funny language.

Over the years the community service group has donated over $76,000 to local charities.

The Beautification and Garden ladies have performed service to the town by designing gardens in the parkway and keeping Town Hall

*Culinary delights are always available at the Taster's Tea.*

grounds planted with seasonal flower and plant arrangements.

The Four Arts group have regular outings to museums, art galleries and theatres, as well as bringing cultural events to the monthly meetings.

A unique fundraiser was conducted by the main Seasiders organization in December of 1960. At the time there was no ambulance service in the area. Palm Beach Shores, Riviera Beach, Lake Park and North Palm Beach donated $700 and the Intercity First Aid Squad was born. The local grocery store, Grator Gator was at the time known as the Piggly Wiggly. A one-week campaign was carried out by the Seasiders to have the whole island shop there and in return a portion of each sale was donated to the Seasiders who in turn donated the proceeds to the squad to help purchase an ambulance.

In 1955 Mrs. Ruth Douglass (President 1958-60) and Mrs. Howe convinced the Seasiders to sponsor a Nativity Scene. The original was made with stenciled wooden figures and located at the palm frond covered Beach Pavilion. Over the summer months paper-mache figures were crafted and clothed so that for the next season an almost life-sized replica was displayed. This time it was to be found at the fountain on the Parkway. The cradle and Joseph's staff where crafted from driftwood found on the beach. In 1960 it found a home at the Town Hall parking lot, where it reappeared every year until 2002. From its inception through the early 80s, Mrs. Douglass repaired and clothed the figures and then Jean Emens carried on the tradition until the Seasiders Board decided to no longer sponsor the display. This "politically correct" decision was made in 2002. So after a run of 47 years, a genuine town tradition came to an end.

In 2004 a non-affiliated group of ladies requested permission to place a smaller crèche on town property and the Town Commission

*Seasiders Ladies display their flower arranging skills.*

readily agreed.

Louise James was a Charter Member of the organization but somehow avoided being President until finally in 1992 she was convinced to serve a two-year term, which she did with distinction.

The Seasiders, with their four groups are not only still very active in Palm Beach Shores, but are one of the main driving forces in the town.

*Mad Hatters luncheon gets everyone in the act.*

# Singer Island Business Association

From the first sales in 1949 the town grew quickly. The push to draw non-retirees, with owner-operated small apartments, was especially successful. By the mid-50's there were 37 such buildings catering to the winter tourist. Their biggest problem was letting the world know where our town was located. The same complaint can still be heard 55 years later when Singer Island, not a municipality and with no post office designation, can not be found on any, but a local area, map. Many of the 30-plus apartment owners joined the Riviera Beach Chamber of Commerce who, for the most part, represented businesses located on the mainland. However, when the Chamber wanted to install a small billboard advertising local accommodations, the Palm Beach Shores members objected. Following a regular Town Commission meeting in 1959 an organizational meeting was held. Mayor Henry Pearson announced plans for the formation of a town chamber. He said the new organization would be divorced from the town, but he offered the use of the Town Hall for meetings and assured the group that they would have full cooperation from the commission.

He asked those present to appoint a Chairman and allowed Mr. Doyle, the only nominee, to conduct the discussion. Doyle explained why a new chamber was a necessity. It seemed that the Riviera Chamber wanted to install a new sign on US 1 advertising local businesses. They requested the Town of Palm Beach Shores to help finance this endeavor. The problem was that the lettering for Riviera Beach was at least four times larger than the letters for Palm Beach Shores. The Town Commission balked at the request and the Riviera Beach Chamber went public with some disparaging remarks, hence the organizational meetings. Mr. Doyle pointed out that the Shores could install their own sign, "in a better location, eight times as large and it will cost no more than what they want us to pay for their sign."

Thus, on that Monday evening in September of 1959, the Palm Beach Shores Chamber of

Commerce was born, with 25 business owners signing up.

A year later it was determined that a separate chamber was not necessary and that more could be accomplished by working with a larger group. Members voted to disband the town's chamber and rejoin Rivera Beach.

This decision was also predicated on the formation of a new local business organization — the Palm Beach Shores Businessmen's Association. In a March 1964 letter to members from President Marion Leaming (owner of a motel, the original Sea Spray, at the north end of the existing Marriott's property and later to build the Best Western Seaspray Hotel) reported on the association's new large signs installed at the north end of the island and also that the Colonnades Hotel was overbooked for a cancer research symposium and requesting members to come forward if they had any vacancies.

The number of apartments in town stayed about the same in the next few years but the rest of the island continued to expand. More motels and apartments just to the north opened and they also joined the association. By 1967 the name had been changed to the Singer Island Businessmen's Association reflecting the continued growth north of Blue Heron Blvd. For the next 40 years a brochure featuring local business establishments was produced and distributed.

The early brochures give an idea of the difference in the service to the tourist as compared to visitors today. The Bon Aire in 1959 advertised their services, which included

*The town had its own Chamber of Commer of Commerce for a little more than a year.*

*SIBA sponsored hockey was televised in northeast U.S. and Canada.*

picking up their clients at the train station and returning them after they had enjoyed their vacation in Paradise. One car families were the norm and parking in town was not a concern. Nowadays, with three cars not unusual, parking has become the town's number one problem. With many visitors coming from the Northeast, most of the bookings were for longer time periods. A three to eight week stay was usual.

The Singer Island Business Association (aka S.I.B.A.) remained an organization made up of and representing the small motel/apartment owner through the rest of the century. At first the only competition was that among themselves, later from the increasing number of brand name hotel/motels on the island then from the large influx of high rise condos. Many owners found it easier to cater to permanent tenants rather than go for a high price winter cliental and empty rooms in the summer. Many did not keep up with the modernization of their units over the years and could no longer compete for a good class of tourist trade. The association volunteers worked hard to address these and other problems as they were identified. The membership fees along with the moneys collected for the annual brochure advertising kept S.I.B.A. going but fundraisers were a necessity in later years. Monthly information meetings kept members up to date and gave them a chance to compare notes with their compatriots. A monthly newsletter was sent when the monthly meetings failed to draw members. The newsletters expanded from one page to a very informative booklet and back again over the years. S.I.B.A. came up with a telephone reference service that would allow each member to register their vacancies with a volunteer who would answer a toll free number. The system was successful in the early years, but like any such system, it was subject to the integrity and dedication of those taking the calls.

The large hotels were always looked upon with suspicion of being unfair competition and were discouraged from membership for many years. When the number of active mom and pop operators had dropped to a number where keeping S.I.B.A. going was becoming very difficult, the plan changed and the large properties were finally encouraged to participate. This move actually saved the organization and the smaller properties since the big hotels added to the ad programs and opened the doors to other promotions. An example was one promoted by the Palm Beach County Tourist Development Board using tax payer dollars. This avenue had been previously explored, unsuccessfully over the years by S.I.C.A. Many social affairs were combined with fundraising and were heavily attended by the town residents not only to support their neighbors but as a welcome entertainment. One of the most memorable was the End of an Era

*Selling the beautiful beach was the easy part of S.I.B.A. promotion to attract tourist to the town.*

cook-out and souvenirs sale during the demolition of the Colonnades.

This was the only organized celebration of the hotel that had played such an outstanding part of the town's history.

Making Singer Island known to northern potential tourists was the main challenge of S.I.B.A. over the years and numerous attempts were made. Russ Sanders, General Manager of the Best Western Hotel distributed free drink wooden nickels in the brochures one year. The idea was to track the effectiveness of the very costly mailings. He proved the point when the return was less than one half of a one percent usage. Probably the project that got the word out best at the least cost was a far out idea for a South Florida organization… hockey!

At the time there was no professional hockey or hockey news in the area, but there were many retired NHL players. Some played in a league in Pompano. Local players who wanted to play had to make an hour plus trek to get to the arena. Denis Heron was the Conference Manager at the Holiday Inn, on the island, at the time. Denis had been not just a goal tender in the NHL but had won the Vesina Trophy as the best goalie in the league. The Holiday Inn, the Buccaneer, the Best Western, the Sailfish and Cannonsport Marinas all contributed to sponsor the Singer Island Mariners. The first exhibition game was held in the West Palm Beach auditorium in 1993 featuring the Singer Island Mariners vs the NHL All Stars. The next year the Mariners played to a capacity crowd when they hosted the Boston Bruins' alumni team. Three members of the American Olympic winning team were present as well as a total of five Hockey Hall of Fame members.

The local press did not employ hockey sports writers at the time and the local publicity was nothing special, but both the English and French Canadian sports networks televised the game as well as the pre- and post-game publicity in the Boston area. The Singer Island name was being repeatedly mentioned. Advertising success! The fans were not disappointed either. Being able to see hockey greats like Bobby Orr and Davy Keon in person was a real treat for displaced hockey fans living in the hockey wilderness of Palm Beach. Both games were played for the Singer Island Challenge Cup, a four foot high trophy donated by the Best Western Hotel and presented by the S.I.B.A. President Meagan Lucksinger.

Most of the original apartments are gone or have changed their names with new owners, but some remain, upgraded and modern yet still possessing the charm of the early designs. Some even retained the '50s two-color tiled bathrooms and enjoyed the return of that style as part of the back to the "good old days" renaissance. A few of the originals remaining would include the Anchorage and the Romaine. The Romaine was the first completed mom and pop apartment complex and was used in one of Mr. Edwards' early sales advertisements.

By the early 2000s the land value of the small properties far exceeded the value of the business located there. One, then another, sold to developers who would change the use of the land from rentals to condo or town home ownership. While the number of rental units decreased, the town was rewarded with a new clientele of owners, not renters, who took a stronger pride in community and provided an increased tax base. S.I.B.A. carried on, but only with the support of businesses that they had formerly banned as members, e.g., large properties and off island concerns. In fact, these members now outnumbered the "mom and pops" that at one time had been the organization's backbone.

*Many homeowners first visited as tourist lured here by S.I.B.A. promotion.*

# Singer Island Civic Association

The Singer Island Civic Association, while not a town organization, has historically had a strong membership representation by town residents. In 1967 spot zoning was being proposed by the Riviera Beach City Council that would allow several high rise buildings and a shopping center on the property now known as Sugar Sands. Area residents formed a committee to organize opposition to the proposal. The ground swell included all the existing residential areas and businesses on the island. Jerry (Jerome) Kelly who was Mr. MacArthur's real estate man and who, with his brothers had developed Yacht Harbor Manor, was instrumental in obtaining legal counsel and later the help of two city planners. The mettle of the group was proven almost immediately when the developer, Continental Con-Dev Corporation, sued the association for over a million dollars. The suit went on for month (others for years). The developer finally gave up but not before he actually started construction of the project.

At times the membership reached over 1,400. S.I.C.A. has been responsible for pushing the drive for a highrise bridge over the intracoastal waterway, getting the beached Greek freighter, the Amaryllis, removed and, although not successful in stopping the 42-story Tiara from being built, they did succeed in having the allowable density significantly reduced. Later they raised $30,000 for legal fees to protect a small lake on the island from developers.

Years later the organization took a decidedly different tack. With the decay and decline of the city it was determined that a sacrifice of the island residents was required to insure the revitalization of the mainland city. This action led to a four-fold increase in density and the influx of row upon row of highrise buildings obliterating the oceanfront, including one over the little lake that the $30,000 had been raised to protect. The idea being that the massive increase of property tax would finance major redevelopment programs on the mainland. This controversial action split the membership and many heated meetings took place.

When S.I.C.A.'s agenda changed 180 degrees from its original direction some members left and formed a new group to protect the livability of the island. This group calls itself Citizens for Responsible Growth in Riviera Beach and its first success was in getting the density of one on the new developments substantially reduced. They also challenged the ability of the bridge and the island's single road to handle the traffic the high-rises will bring. Despite being divided, SICA is still a major voice in city politics.

*The S.I.C.A. has worked for the betterment of the island for both home and condo owners for many years.*

# The Old Bastards

The most unique organization in the town would have to be the "Old Bastards." This group of men meet at the Top of the Spray restaurant, reserving the big round tables, overlooking the ocean, on a weekly basis to discuss and resolve the problems of the world.

Hank Gardner started the group sometime around 1988 (no one seems to be able to remember exactly when); and he would start each meeting by exclaiming, "what a beautiful view." The organization was not concerned with details; no by-laws, no officers, no dues, but lots of opinions. The original members were Hank, Bill Tremain, Bill Kellner, Ken Wagenbach, Tom Mills, Tom Chilcote, Jim Rielly, George Sylvester, John Bohney and Frank Wladich. They referred to themselves as the "Old Bastards."

It was a surprise to all when Jim Reilly showed up with membership cards for each member from the "International Organization of Old Bastards." This over a million member club even had its own motto, "Illegitmos Non Carbrundum Est" or "don't let the bastards get you down." Frank Wladich (Retired Colonel New Jersey State Trooper) returned from a Police Chiefs' convention with matching windbreakers for the O.B.s (as they were referred to in polite company). The jackets were worn with pride no matter how hot the weather. The meetings went on for years without problems, but when Bill Kellner died in 1997 his sister included in his obituary, along with his Knights of Columbus and Kiwanis affiliations, his membership in the Singer Island Chapter of the International Organization of Old Bastards. That peaked the curiosity of newspaper reporter Ron Hayes and he invited himself, along with a photographer, to join the group for lunch. The ensuing front page article in the Accent section of the Palm Beach Post resulted in the members being barraged with would be recruits. Being true Old Bastards they secretly moved the time of the luncheon. When that did not work they changed the day and finally the meeting place. One outsider, Ransford Triggs, was so persistent and so interesting that he was finally granted membership.

At a recent meeting in 2006 the attendees were George Sylvester, Tom Chilcote, Tom Mills, Frank Wladich, Peter Farley, Howard Rourke and Art Donelan. Rans Triggs, at 96 years of age, was looking forward to the meeting, but the night before fell and broke his femur. Unfortunately, Rans did not survive the resulting hospital stay. Only four of the original ten members make it to the luncheon. However, it does not seem to be a problem to find town residents that qualify to be accepted as an "Old Bastard."

*A much younger Old Bastard Rans Triggs, described as the foremost marksman in America in this Life Magazine cover advertisement for Camel cigarettes.*

# Colonnades

Water mains, hydrants, marinas, docks and streets were the signs that a major development was becoming a reality. Mr. Edwards started work on his Inlet Court Hotel before the road paving had been completed. This rambling 2-story oceanfront structure was completed in early 1949 and reportedly enjoyed a full house for the 1949-50 winter season. It was grand by the area's standards at the time and included an Olympic size swimming pool with adjacent kiddy pool, oceanview dinning room, and on-the-ocean dining patio. The architecture featured columns supporting the second floor walkways and patios giving a very "open living" atmosphere, just right for northerners dreaming of tropical vacations. Mr. Edwards soon realized the name Inlet Court sounded like a transient motel rather than a destination resort and changed the name to The Colonnades.

The hotel was featured in all of the sales brochures and advertising for the new development called Palm Beach Shores. Property buyers were promised access to the swimming club and use of the dining room for parties. It became the meeting place for all the social and community service clubs in the area. Having dinner at the Colonnades was the "in thing" in the '50s and '60s.

Edwards' plan for the hotel was to create a center point for his development. He had no intention of staying in the hotel business,

*Inlet Court Hotel, later the Colonnades. This 1954 view shows the hotel complex as completed by Mr. Edwards.*

*Inlet Court Hotel under construction in November of 1948. Note the palm trees planted along streets.*

*Colonnades Inlet Court Hotel. Postcards showing view of Beach Balcony; view of columns supporting patios and second story walkways and entrance to Yacht Club.*

*Colonnades in 1963. Note Convention Center building on right.*

although his previous experience proved him to be an expert in the field. In 1951 he sold the hotel to a successful group who had created the Bahia Mar in Ft. Lauderdale. They could not make a go of it and he repossessed it in 1952 for non-payment. He still owned it in 1960 when he died and the hotel, along with all his other land holdings, became part of his estate. The lands he held in Palm Beach Shores were in the name of Colonnades Inc., which was the holding legality for the beach, the parkway, the public thoroughfares, etc.

Included in the 1951 sale was the Palm Beach Shores Yacht Club and the Club House on Lake Drive (the Buccaneer). This became known as the Bahia Mar Yacht Club. The name stayed around for quite some time after the repossession of the hotel itself.

In 1963 a new developer hit the local scene. John D. MacArthur was very successfully developing Palm Beach Gardens and the championship PGA golf courses. Edwards' estate offered the hotel to John D, who thought it was a bargain at $800,000. Mr. MacArthur appeared before the Town Commission and said he wanted to be a good neighbor. Unfortunately, the town citizens did not see eye to eye with his ideas and five years of accusations, law suits and animosity ensued. Without the benefit of permits, the buildings grew from sprawling two-story structures to seven stories with over 400 rooms. Construction was complete in 1968. Until it was condemned in 1987 it was without doubt the north county social center and the only 3 (and 4) star hotel.

Construction of the hotel additions were made with an eye to cutting corners and cost savings. Engineering problems continually cropped up using band-aid fixes to remedy them. The original existing buildings were never designed to bear the weight of these additions of new floors. This would eventually be the cause of the hotel's demise. In the meantime, proms, graduations, weddings, swimming competitions, service club meetings, national beauty contest and even dog shows all

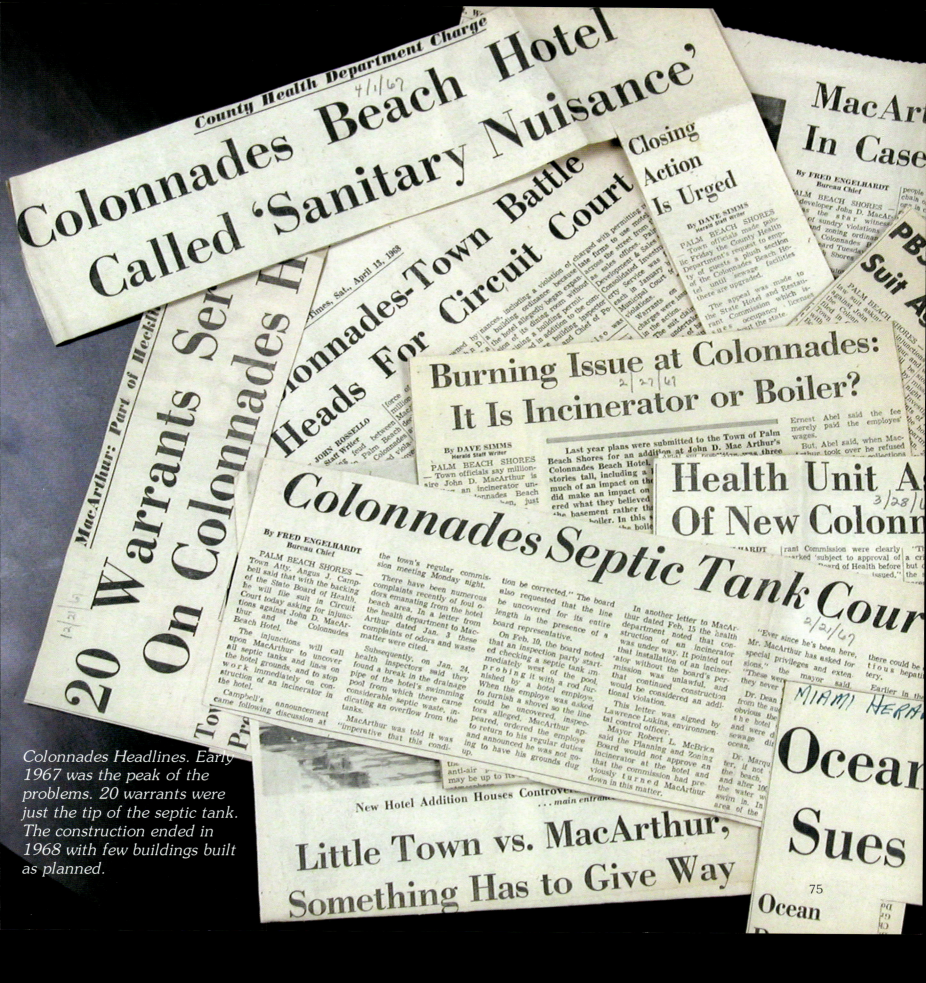

*Colonnades Headlines. Early 1967 was the peak of the problems. 20 warrants were just the tip of the septic tank. The construction ended in 1968 with few buildings built as planned.*

*Colonnades Entrance View. The hotel did look good! When big named guests arrived, town complaints became fewer.*

*A few surprised guests watch a 650 lb American Black Bear with a boy on its back enter the Colonnades lobby. But it was just Gentle Ben, star of his own TV show.*

vied for this beautiful venue. At times, when a formal dance with a big band was in full swing, couples dressed in tuxedoes and ballroom gowns would catch a display of the moon rising out of the horizon against the silver waters of the Atlantic Ocean. A more idyllic spot did not exist.

The main dining room was built on three tiers centered by a huge aquarium. A claim of serving more than 200 dinners on a summer night when other establishments were empty, and a Sunday evening buffet stretching from the lobby front doors to the center of the room, attested to its popularity.

The bar was built as a carousel and rotated 360 degrees every hour. The locals came with their out of town visitors to catch a glimpse of celebrities that stayed there regularly or they came just to see Mr. MacArthur feed his famous ducks. The celebrity list included names recognized from Hollywood, radio, television and even the Supreme Court. Bob Hope, Bing Crosby, Jackie Gleason, Jack Nicolas, Lee Trevino, Paul Harvey, Mike Wallace, Jesse Jackson, Chief Justice Warren Burger, Burt Reynolds, Elizabeth Taylor, AL Martino, Helen Hayes, Vera Miles, Cliff Robertson, H.L. Hunt, Morton Downey Sr., Burgess Meredith, Perry

*Colonnades Lagoon. Home of the TV show "Treasure Island," the Lagoon was known coast to coast.*

Como, Anthony Quinn, Billy Graham, Dennis Weaver, Janis Joplin and the Rolling Stones all stayed at the Colonnades in this quiet little town.

Glenn Aitkins, Fire Inspector for the town, recalls his teenage experience as a keybord player in a local band. The band was playing for a wedding reception at the hotel when Janis Joplin dropped in to listen. She was followed shortly by the keyboard man for Three Dog Night, who came up and showed Glenn how to improve on one of the Three Dog Night's songs he was playing.

The best room in the house was the Bob Hope suite, built as a penthouse on top of the main building. Entrance was gained via a flight of stairs from the sixth floor elevators. Double doors opened onto an outdoor deck area complete with a fountain. The suite included a huge ornate bed, a bathroom shower with nine shower heads, and a sunken tub with brass fixtures. A built-in bar was a necessity, but the grand piano, once owned by Irving Berlin, was a very special feature.

The most private rooms were on the 7th floor of the Paradise Building where Mr.

General Manager Ron Kairella was very popular and a good friend to the town. A power failure led to his death shortly after this picture was taken.

Colonnades Before Demolition. A view of the empty hotel waiting for a buyer.

Colonnades Demolition. With "End of an Era" celebration, the Grand Old Lady of Palm Beach Shores crumbles to the ground.

MacArthur and his wife Catherine made their home. It had a grand view of the parking lot and was decorated in early Sears, non-matching furniture.

Stories are still told of Jackie Gleason's drinking to excess, including the time he passed out and his face fell into his dinner. The story goes that the waitress simply lifted his head up, removed the dinner, and gently put his head back on the table. Janis Joplin, during one stay, reportedly skinny dipped in the swimming pool.

On a Friday afternoon in June 1967 heads turned when the lobby doors opened and in lumbered a 660-pound black bear with a 67-pound boy in tow. The bear was "Gentle Ben," the star of a new TV series being produced by Ivan Tors in Miami. The boy was child star Clint Howard, brother of future noted director/actor Ron Howard. The show was shooting off Bee Line Highway just south of Monet Road. The occasion for their visit to the Colonnades was for a publicity pitch for the prime time show that preceded the Ed Sullivan Show on Sunday night. The top rated series was a follow-up to Tors Television Productions' previous hit "Flipper" and starred Vera Miles and Dennis Weaver as the boy's parents. Needless to say, stars, extras and crew all stayed at the Colonnades while they were in Palm Beach County.

One of the more well-known stories of the hotel occurred during a visit from Bob Hope. Mr. Hope had ordered a room service breakfast and then got on the phone. Room service arrived. He gestured for the server to just put it down beside the bed. Instead the waiter started to pour the coffee causing Hope to loudly object before he realized that the waiter was Mr. MacArthur. At that moment the hotel photographer entered the room and snapped a picture of a pajama clad, tousled Hope taking a cup from a towel-over-the-arm MacArthur. The picture was a hotel treasure for years.

Even after the closing of the hotel, Burt Reynolds used the Oceanside Tiki Bar as his office for his popular TV detective series, B.L. Stryker.

Although MacArthur had a reputation for furnishing the Colonnades with dinnerware and other necessities from other hotels that had gone out of business, he did have some genuine treasures.

The lobby had a life size, hand-carved sleigh complete with horse from Poland Imperial days, as well as giant size vases from the Ming Dynasty.

After Macarthur's death in January 1978, the hotel operated for years (without the ducks) and enjoyed a good reputation. The co-operation with the town was at an all time high. Residents were invited to use the pool and offered discounts for food and drinks. The new General Manager, Ron Kairalla, was a young man who had been in the MacArthurs' employ for many years. He was a local boy who started work as the hotel lifeguard. He was very well liked and worked hard and successfully to attract foreign tourists and to build rapport with the locals. For the town's Christmas caroling hayride he not only supplied the wagon and hay but supplied, at his expense, two very popular musicians, who were often booked by the hotel (Steve and Angela) to provide music and to lead the singing.

For the 4th of July, Kairalla planned an extravaganza complete with fireworks and invited the whole town to attend. The feature performer was Arlo Guthrie. A few days before the event, the town suffered one of its many power failures. The established hotel procedure under power outage was for key employees to check each floor for guests stuck in elevators. Ron took the fourth floor and apparently opened the elevator doors to check the position of the elevator. He lost his balance and tragically fell to his death.

The 4th of July celebration went on as planned. Ron would have been very proud of its success. It turned out to be a testimonial for his community involvement.

The end of the Colonnades era came about in an ironic way. Sheriff Richard Wille was hosting the Florida Police Chief's conference, one of the many first class conventions held annually at the hotel. The cocktail hour was coming to an end and dinner was announced. As the attendees started to enter the second floor dinning room, a loud groan was heard, the floor dropped and tables tipped over. The main support beam had given way. An area of the floor was supported only by the cast iron pipes located in the ceiling of the kitchen below. A follow-up building inspection determined that the hotel was not safe. After a short legal battle the total complex closed in 1987 and never re-opened. Attempts were made to sell and rumors spread that a new buyer was prepared to rejuvenate it, but they never proved to be anything but rumors.

After years of no activity the town forced the issue and in 1990 the "Grand Old Lady" of Palm Beach Shores, including the original Inlet Court dining room, the Carousel Bar, the Bob Hope Suite and MacArthur's small apartment, came crashing to the ground as nothing more than a pile of dust and debris. The land sat vacant until 1999 when the first of the Marriott buildings was completed.

*Colonnades , 1970, from the ocean.*

# Buildings

## The Blue Heron Hotel

The first building of note on the island was Mr. Singer's Blue Heron Hotel, which was started in 1926, never finished, and demolished in 1940. Also in 1940, the Town of Riviera Beach purchased their ocean front beach.

## Steen's Restaurant

In May, 1941 Riviera Beach leased a 100' x 100' section of the beach to a gentleman named Ryder Steen. Steen's Restaurant stayed in business for over a quarter of a century. In the beginning there was no water, no electricity, no deliveries and no garbage pick-up. During the war years many servicemen from Morrison Field or other nearby military bases visited the island and enjoyed lunch at Steen's. The bridge from the mainland, not in the best of shape to begin with, suffered further deterioration by an increase of traffic. More than one bridge fire was put out by hauling buckets of water on a long rope, from the lake below. The Steen's welcomed Mr. Edwards and his Palm Beach Shores development since it meant water, electricity, roads and a new bridge. In 1956 the Steen's bought a lot on Inlet Way where they built a home and became long term town residents.

## The Colonnades

The Inlet Court Hotel was the next building of consequence to the town. Started in 1948, it was the center for town affairs throughout its days as the Inlet Court, briefly as the Bahia Mar and best known as the Colonnades. This building is a major part of the town's history detailed in the chapter beginning on page 70.

## The Romaine

The first apartment building in town was located at the corner of Cascade and Ocean. This building was shown in early ads both when under construction and when finished, but the building that Mr. Edwards put in all his brochures after it was completed was the Romaine Apartments located on Inlet Way. The Romaine is important for two reasons, first because it was featured in the sales brochures as an example of a successful mom and pop operation and second because the owner

*Mayor Wolfe lays cornerstone for Mayan Tower Building.*

turned out to be the town's longest residing inhabitants, Louise and George James, who now live on Claremont Lane.

*The bridge was rebuilt the same year this photo was taken (1935). John Woolley, age 4, along with his father were two of the few visitors to the island. This was the same year that a youngster fell to his death from the building. Note that the top two floors are missing from the original structure.*

## The Buccaneer

The Buccaneer Restaurant and Bar, originally the Palm Beach Shores Yacht Club, was built on the lakefront before 1950. It was featured in all of the early brochures, and in the third edition of sales promotions, pictured as a gathering place for new residents and visiting boaters. When Mr. Edwards sold the Colonnades Hotel in 1951 to the Ft. Lauderdale Bahia Mar developer, the Colonnades name was changed to the Bahia Mar and the Yacht Club was part of the sale.

The property was taken back for non-payment and the Colonnades name returned to the hotel on the ocean, but the Yacht Club retained the name Bahia Mar for a long time afterwards. It quickly became the favorite watering hole for the developer's real estate salesmen and local residents alike. This reputation continued through many owners and, in fact, was still well earned when it closed in 2004. In the mid-1970s Actor Bert Lahr, famous for his role as the cowardly lion in the stage play and movie "Wizard of Oz," ate dinner every night at the "Buc." His regular order was a bowl of split pea soup with no salt but lots of MSG.

Although all the docks were privately used, an International Yacht Club was chartered and conducted the Buccaneer Invitational Fishing Tournaments for over thirty years. This prestigious contest drew fishermen from all parts of the country.

The Buccaneer was the building in town with the most serious sewage problem. Their septic tanks would overflow on a busy night even without a rainfall. Many a weekend night a pump out truck would be parked in the fire lane and put to use more than once during the evening.

The original building was expanded by building rental apartments without providing adequate parking. This was the start of a serious problem at this location and one which would later be seen in other parts of town, growing over time to become the town's largest single concern. The apartments were later converted to condominiums creating a very unusual circumstance. The bar and restaurant were retained as one condo. Problems, including parking and noise, began immediately between this one unit owner and the other seventeen.

## The Beach Club

The Beach Club building sat where the Palm Beach Shores Resort is today. It was a small cocktail lounge and package store frequented mostly by mainlanders, although it had a small

*Belmar Motel Apartments later known as the George then the Islander and finally the Channel House.*

following of town folks. The Club existed for the late night crowd and had a 3 am closing hour. The building could not compete with more and more newer establishments opening as the island grew. It survived a fire caused by one of the neon beer signs, but still closed and sat vacant for years before ironically being burnt to the ground, as part of a Volunteer Fire Department drill.

## The Seaspray Hotel

Marion Leaming had a small, one-story motel to the north of the Colonnades and just to the south of the entrance road to the beach. In the early '60s he received a permit to add a second story, increasing the number of units to 30. The newly completed building was sold to John MacArthur in 1972 and became part of the Colonnades Hotel. Mr Leaming purchased the lots on the north side of the beach road and in July of 1966 broke ground for a 50-unit extension of his motel to be operated under a Best Western franchise. The building, built as it is seen today with an estimated cost of $500,000, featured underground parking and private balconies for each large room. The artist renditions forgot to show the town's beach parking lot. Instead, it had the Best Western bordering directly on the beach. Mr. and Mrs. Phil Bowser purchased the hotel in 1978, which is still part of the Best Western family. The Leamings were both active in tourism promotion with the Palm Beach Shores Chamber of Commerce, the Riviera Beach Chamber, The Palm Beach Shores Businessman Association, and the Singer Island Businessman Association. The Bowsers continue to be actively involved in local business organizations.

## Palm Beach Shores Apartments

The building at 33 Ocean, the Palm Beach Shores Apartments, not only was the "talk of the town" when it was built, it was also the tallest. Its gracious design and features, such as an ocean view for every unit, proved to be extremely desirable over the years. It was the forerunner of modern day condos. The apartments were sold with "co-op" ownership. The original brochure advertised short-term rentals being available, but this ended shortly after the units were all sold.

## The Mayan Towers

Dr. Vecchione had the first of 240 concrete pilings driven in the ground in 1968 for his $2 million condo building just north of the Best Western and the public beach. He announced that this was the first phase of a $5 million development to be built on adjoining lots. The original building was eight stories high, with dimensions of 64 feet wide by 333 feet long sitting on two lots, totaling 150 feet by 550 feet deep. The apartments would sell for from $20,000 to $40,000 with unit size ranging 1,000 square feet for the one bedroom, 1 1/2 bath model and 1,500 for the two bedroom, two bath model.

The building was built with a site elevation lower than the surrounding area and suffered from extensive flooding in the garage, game room, and lobby. In the late 1980s a manual pump system was installed so that the excess water could be pumped out of the parking lot drains before the water could rise to the flood level. This system was only used during storms with very heavy rains and a few years went by without it being turned on. During Hurricane Frances in 2004 the town was deluged with water. New people were involved with the building management and were unaware of the pumping system. Once again, the lobby flooded. Some egg-on-face was detected when it was discovered that the system existed and

*After many years of discussion the Community Center groundbreaking finally took place in January, 2006.*

could be put back into operation relatively easily.

Mayan Tower II, also known as Mayan North, was built soon after the completion of Tower I, on the lots immediately north of the first building. This time the correct base elevation was used. The second building was much larger and also enjoyed immediate sales success. In 1974 the Mayan North sued the builder for poor workmanship causing the 5-year-old roof to be replaced and the Mayan South had to install booster pumps because the top three floors could not get water from the taps when water demand was high.

The two buildings have many year-round residents who represent a good share of the town's voting population.

*1966 promo rendition of the Best Western Seaspray. Town's parking lot, between building and beach, has disappeared!*

## Town Hall

The landmark building in Palm Beach Shores is the Town Hall building. The New England style design of a small meeting place seems to typify the character of the town, i.e., small, picturesque, well designed, and rooted in a spirit of volunteerism. The building originated as the construction shack during the development phase of the town. The original building included just the meeting room. The shack was used for material and vehicle storage. The southern part of the floor has a pronounced decline towards the street, as all good garages should. This slope resulted in the unique design of the pattern of the floor tile during the 2005 renovations. Also a service ramp used to change vehicle oil, etc., was found stored in the roof framing. It was left in place both due to its historic significance and due to the cost involved in removing and rebuilding the rafter system required to get it out. If it managed to stay hidden for more than 55 years, why break its secret?

With the change of the building function from storage shack to building office to Town Hall, the original room was partitioned to include both offices and meeting room. The steeple was added and in the '60s the original building was expanded with the addition of the two-story structure behind the original. In this new addition, the ground floor provided a new home for the Public Works Department while the second story housed the building officials' office and records storage area. The unusual feature was a one bedroom apartment for the use of the town's Police Sergeant. The apartment was used by the staff and police as an office when no longer needed as housing. This second story was used through the '80s. In the 1990s a major addition to the building was made extending the original ground floor to the east creating ample office space while enlarging the meeting room and creating a full kitchen. The upstairs fell into a state of disrepair and was used only for storage. In 2004-05 the building was remodeled. With new air conditioning and carpeting the upstairs portion became the most sought after office space in the building. The building is structurally sound and will hopefully continue to be the town's focal point and source of pride for another 50 years.

## Police Annex

One of the original buildings in town was built to house the heavy equipment for the water system. Construction took place in 1947 and, along with the 300,000 gallon water tank, preceded other structures. The building has a three-foot thick foundation that supported the very large motors, pumps and generators. This cement block building withstood 50 years of storm abuse, and a decade of neglect. When the equipment and the tank became obsolete, the town bought the land, building and tank from Riviera Beach for $55,000. The tank was torn down and a park created on the land. The building was repaired and upgraded and now serves as a Police Annex and has proven through numerous hurricanes that it can withstand whatever nature throws at it.

The newest addition to the town's building inventory will be the Community Center, located at the beach. This Center will take some of the pressure off of the Town Hall meeting room and allow for larger town functions. After being talked about for more than 20 years, ground was broken on January 28, 2006.

Newer buildings include the Captain's Walk on Lake Drive (condo), The Inlet Beach Club on Inlet Way, (condo). The Embassy Suites renamed Radisson (hotel) and later turned into time share units as the Palm Beach Shores Resort on Ocean Avenue, the largest tax payer in town, the Marriott time share buildings on Ocean Avenue. Under construction are a beautiful oceanfront condo on Ocean Avenue called the Dolce Vita, a smaller rendition on Inlet Way with the same name, Cannonsport Marina and condos on Lake Drive and the Sailfish Marina condos also on Lake. The mom and pop apartment motels of the 1950s are being replaced with new modern attractive buildings all helping to keep Palm Beach Shores the "Best Little Town in Florida."

33 Ocean. Palm Beach Shores Apartments, first condo co-op in town.

1948. First multi family buildng under construction. Cascade and Ocean.

The beach club, located where the Palm Beach Shores Resort now stands, was a popular late night lounge.

# Auto Races

The racing world press covered the race extensively and one of the best accounts was found in the program of the 1986 Grand Prix of Palm Beach. This article is presented as written with only minor corrections and updates. Authorship has not been able to be established, therefore apologies are extended for not being able to give credit where credit is certainly due.

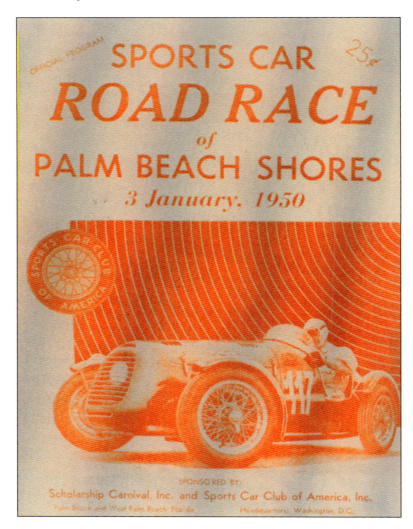

On January 3, 1950 the Sports Car Club of America held what is accepted as being the first international road race in the United States. It was the first time a Jaguar competed in the U.S., the first time an American motor race was held in the rain, and the first time a race was won on white wall tires! And it took place in the little town of Palm Beach Shores. Here's how it all happened:

The prelude to the race was a 1,300 mile sports car rally. Although the point of origin was in New York City, many of the 20 entries joined the rally in Boston, Chicago, Detroit and Washington D.C. This three-day event ended at the Biltmore Hotel in Palm Beach on New Year's Eve.

It was a windy, rainy morning at Palm Beach Shores on January 3rd, 1950. But that did not stop over 25,000 people from gathering to watch America's first sports car street race. The Palm Beach Shores Road Race made history that day, a huge success by all accounts. But it was a race that almost didn't happen, and was held only one more time.

Over 34 years have passed since the Palm Beaches last hosted a major auto racing event. A look back to the origins of American road racing shows the heritage the Grand Prix of Palm Beach shares with the Palm Beach Shores event years before.

Following the Second World War, foreign cars were quite a novelty in America. An Alfa-Romeo, Fiat, Ferrari, Jaguar or MG was a strange sight, and finding parts or someone who would attempt to repair them was nearly impossible. A small group of enthusiasts formed, called the Sports Car Club of America (SCCA), a carry-over of the old Automobile Racing Club of America which was active during the 1930s. Their goal was to promote road racing and "sports cars" in the U.S. to the same degree of success enjoyed in Europe.

Many of the early sports car enthusiasts lived in the Palm Beaches, so it was only natural that West Palm Beach would be an excellent site for America's first street race through a resort town's business and shopping district. The SCCA had already staged successful events on the country roads of Watkins Glen, NY, as well as Bridgehampton on Long Island. The West Palm Beach race was to be something special, however.

Wealthy land developer Miles Collier, his brother Sam, and Palm Beach resident Phil Stiles were the chief organizers of what was to be called the "Round the Houses Road Race of the Palm Beaches."

The event was scheduled to take place along a scenic 1.98 mile course that ran down Flagler Drive past the West Palm Beach Marina, Flagler Park, and the Hotel Pennsylvania to just past the South Bridge, then west to Olive Avenue where the cars would race north to 5th Street and then back east to Flagler. The pits were to be located across from the marina.

Since the SCCA was comprised of amateur sportsmen who did not compete for prize money, the event would be sponsored by a local charity - Scholarship Carnival, Inc., and the SCCA.

Alec Ulmann, chairman of the SCCA's competition activity board, stated that, "This will mark the first time in the United States that a round-the-houses street race has been run through the main shopping area of a city of such size as West Palm Beach."

Ulmann, who would later become famous for promoting the 12 Hours of Sebring, announced a deadline for entries of Dec. 24, 1949. Meanwhile, the city and its merchants were thrilled at the prospects of a Monte Carlo type event taking place.

With a month to go before the historic Round the Houses affair, everything seemed to be going well. Entries were pouring in and the race had already received nationwide publicity. There was trouble on the horizon, however.

Lurking in the shadow of the race's great potential was Sherman (Red) Crise, race promoter who most recently made headlines as the mayor of the infamous speed trap Hacienda Village located on SR 84 west of Ft. Lauderdale. During the 1940s, Crise was a promoter of auto races who apparently felt threatened by SCCA and its amateur race status. Crise, who already had a string of enemies from other ventures, started a campaign to ban auto racing from city streets, with West Palm Beach being his first target. Crise told of possible horror stories — spectator deaths, and warned cities they would be fully responsible for the outcome of such a disaster.

Crise campaigned hard against the race, and the City Commission started to get cold feet. The SCCA assured the city the race would take place without serious incident, but Crise had the backing of other promoters of race tracks and by using scare tactics the city was ready to cancel the event.

With only a couple weeks before the scheduled race, the SCCA decided to take matters into their own hands. Mr. Ullman recalled that A.O. Edwards was developing a subdivision on "homeless" Singer Island and that he was an avid racing fan. In fact, he had developed Grand Prix racing in South Africa before World War II. Mr. Edwards was in favor of using his town, which had brand new streets and very few homes, as the race location thinking the publicity would not hurt future sales. He probably remembered the worldwide publicity his London Grosvenor House hotel received from his sponsorship of the England to Australia Great Air Race a decade earlier. The West Palm Beach race was cancelled and the Palm Beach Shores race was on.

Workmen were put to work in feverish haste, corners were widened and resurfaced, pits and grandstands erected and appropriate cut-out points painted.

The new 2.1 mile circuit was on the rather deserted streets of the town, but no less scenic than the Round the Houses circuit in West Palm Beach. The starting line was on Ocean Avenue at the entrance to the Inlet Court Hotel. Cars would travel down Ocean south to Inlet Way, west to Lake Drive and then north to Island Road, east along Island Road, passing the pits and grandstand where Grator Gator stands today, to Beach Court, south on Beach Court to Beach Road, west on Beach to Park Avenue, south on Park to Bamboo, back east on Bamboo to Ocean then south on Ocean, pass the stands and start and finish lines for the next lap.

It was a beautiful course, though there was only two weeks to prepare it. Admission to the race was $2.50 and the advance ticket sales were going quite well. The change of location did not seem to dampen the enthusiasm of the race fans, but the merchants of West Palm Beach were furious at the City Commission for its lack of firm support for the race. The local paper blasted the city for its "unforgivable display of unadulterated incompetence."

Unlike the massive preparations for the 1986 Grand Prix of Palm Beach, there wasn't a whole lot that needed to be done to the circuit on Singer Island. Some fencing and a lot of sand piles in front of potential hazards, a few hay bales and some roped off areas were enough to prepare for the historic Palm Beach Shores Road Race.

The entries read like a Who's Who in Sports Car Racing for 1950. Briggs Cunningham entered a Cadillac-Healey for the event, while James Kimberly fielded a Jaguar. Others included Bill Spear, Tommy Cole, John Fitch, Phil Walters (also known as Ted Tappett in midget racing circles), Bob Gegen, George Huntoon, George Rand, and stock car racing legend Red Byron.

To usher in the new decade, a special road rally from New York's Henry Hudson Hotel to the Palm Beach Biltmore was held with the cars arriving on New Year's Eve. It was going to be sports car racing's most glamorous event ever held.

Race day, January 3, 1950, was a cool, windy and rainy day. The course was in fine

shape, however, thanks to the $12,000 spent by A.O. Edwards, the developer, to smooth out some of the turns and widen a few other portions of the circuit. A larger than expected crowd flowed onto Singer Island for the Palm Beach Shores Road Race, with spectators lining almost every inch of the way.

*The 1951 race drew almost twice the crowd as the previous race.*

The official Jaguar pace car pulled off the course at 2:05 pm and the green flag was waved starting the Palm Beach Shores Road Race. Thirty-five cars started the race, with the Cadillac-powered Allard of Tommy Cole taking the early lead. (Cole would soon become an internationally recognized sports car driver, but was later killed at Le Mans).

While the cars were competing for overall position in the 50 lap race, the cars were also competing within four different classes depending on engine size.

Taking the lead on the third lap was George Huntoon, driving a car that many disputed could be classified as a "sports car." Huntoon's racer was a former Indianapolis 500 Duesenberg race car with a highly modified Ford engine. Fenders and headlights had been bolted on prior to the race to give the car a more "sports car" appearance. One thing was for certain, it was fast, pulling away from the field with the exception of the Jaguar driven by Leslie Johnson. Johnson had not only just brought his car over from England, but brought his mechanic as well!

As the race progressed, many cars were having brake problems, but there were no major mishaps. Miles Collier in a Ford-Riley, Briggs Cunningham and Bill Milliken in a Bugatti were running in the top five but could not compete with Huntoon's Indy car. Huntoon won the race at an average speed of 57.4 mph, nearly a lap ahead of Briggs Cunningham. George Rand in a Ferrari was third, followed by Johnson's Jaguar and the Healey of Phil Walters. Only 18 cars finished the race.

The first Palm Beach Shores Road Race was a big success, and received excellent media coverage. It was clearly the finest street race yet held in the United States. Plans were started soon after the race for an even bigger event in 1951.

The second annual Palm Beach Shores Road Race was scheduled for December 1951, leaving almost two years between the two races. In that period of time, there were many changes in the fast growing world of sports car racing.

Sam Collier, brother of race founder Miles Collier, was killed at the 1950 Watkins Glen race. New road races had sprung up at locations such as Elkhart Lake, Wisconsin, and Pebble Beach, California. But the biggest development was the fast growing use of airports as a race site. Crowd control was becoming a big problem, and airports were a logical and economical place to stage a road race.

In the two years between the first and second Palm Beach Shores race, Palm Beach Shores grew tremendously. The once empty streets were now lined with new homes, and the circuit became much more difficult to secure.

Auto Sport Magazine wrote in 1952: "When the SCCA ran its first event here two years ago, local real estate development was just beginning. Today, the eye meets row upon row of charmingly designed stucco-type villas in a setting of palms and landscaped gardens. This interesting scene reminds you of the French Riviera."

The December 1951 Palm Beach Shores Road Race was sponsored by the local Kiwanis Club and was divided into five separate races, with the feature being the "Riviera Beach Trophy Race." The course has been altered only slightly since the inaugural event, and still measures about two miles.

Beautiful weather greeted the record crowd estimated at 40,000 to the second annual event. Briggs Cunningham, who now (1986) builds his own cars in downtown West Palm Beach, won the first event of the day, followed by Fritz Koster, John Fitch and Peter Dillnut winning their respective events.

In the main event, John Fitch recorded his second win of the day by powering his Ferrari to an average speed of 60.6 mph to win the glamorous event over Fred Wacker and third place Phil Stiles. George Huntoon, defending champion at Palm Beach Shores, finished sixth driving an Alfa-Romeo.

The race was considered one of the most organized and well attended races in SCCA history, and everyone looked forward to another event the following year, but this was not to be.

*1950. Jaquars XK-120's as pace car and in pole position.*

*Leslie Johnson from London, one of the leading drivers in the U.K., sits behind wheel of his Jaguar XK-120 for photo shoot promoting the 1950 Palm Beach Shores International Road Race. The same car set a world record of 132 mph in the Belgium straightaway race.*

The surrounding area of Singer Island grew too much, and another race would be impossible to hold on the streets of Palm Beach Shores. The SCCA was now looking for airports to stage most of their events. In 1952, two historic events all but insured the end of auto racing on the streets of Singer Island. The SCCA staged a very successful 12 hour endurance sports car race at the Vero Beach Airport in March 1952, followed a week later by Sebring's first 12 hour event, sanctioned by the American Automobile Association. In 1953, MacDill Air Force Base in Tampa would be the site of a major sports car event. Airport racing appeared to have taken over.

Sports car racing all but disappeared in the Palm Beaches for the next 30 years. The Boca Raton Airport (now the Site of Florida Atlantic University) hosted a major sports car event in 1957, and in 1966 Sebring promoter Alec Ulmann announced the famous 12 hour event would be moved to the newly constructed Palm Beach International Raceway (now called Moroso Motorsports Park). Of course, that never happened.

The Bahamas got into the act during the late 1950s and early '60s when none other than Red Crise promoted races at the Nassau Airport.

And what happened to those involved with the original Round the Houses Road Race concept? Sadly, Miles Collier died of polio a short time after his brother was killed at Watkins Glen. Phil Stiles still lives in Palm Beach and has a great interest in antique gas-powered miniature race cars. Briggs Cunningham, who lives in California and has a fabulous museum, went on to a very successful racing career. George Huntoon lives in Naples and enjoys riding his motorcycles, while Alec Ulmann, known as "Mr. Sebring," recently passed away after living in New York, where he was quite active in the world of automobiles. And at last report, Red Crise was residing in the Ft. Lauderdale area.

There were many others who played an important role in the historic Palm Beach Shores Road Races. But the question remains: "What if the race was held in downtown West Palm Beach as originally planned?"

The 1986 Grand Prix of Palm Beach turned out to be an equally historic event. When the Camel GT cars rolled into town, it certainly stirred up some memories of a race that caught the imagination of a young, fast-growing community… which turned out to be the "Best Little Town in Florida."

# Peanut Island

*Peanut Island. The 1917-18 dredged channel that is only 4 feet deep is well defined in this photo. Shoaling near the ocean is seen, as is a small island near what will become the north jetty.*

Pre-1918 photographs show large irregular sand shoals where present day Peanut Island stands. The same photographs show Singer Island loosely connected to Palm Beach by a series of similar shoaling. The Federal Government eventually agreed to allow spoils from the dredging of the new inlet to be placed in the lake. Permission had been previously denied based on "a desire to protect Lake Worth from unnecessary encroachment." An early photo shows the island created by the dredging of the 4-foot deep channel.

In 1926 General George Goethal, the builder of the Panama Canal, was hired to enable all oceangoing vessels to enter the port by engineering an enlargement of the harbor. This included dredging the inlet, as well as the channel from the inlet to the port and the port itself to a depth of 24 feet. The additional dredged sand raised the height of the spoils area well above sea level, creating a permanent island. The planned 24-foot depth was never completed because the bank holding the $3.5 million bonds failed and the project was brought to a standstill.

The new island was originally called Hood's Island in recognition of the first chairman of the Port Commission. It was also known at various times as Inlet Island and Parker Island, for a port worker who once briefly lived on the shoal. There are various stories as to how the island came to be called Peanut Island. One is that a peanut processing plant was proposed to be built on the island to process goobers, which were to be grown on a tract in Belle Glade. Another is that a county commissioner said the island was not worth peanuts and a third legend claimed it was so named because of its peanut-like shape, although early photos certainly do not show this characteristic.

For years local officials requested that the Federal Government commit to a lifeboat rescue station in the vicinity of the inlet. They thought they succeeded when a 1921 bill was approved by Congress, but nothing happened. In 1930 Congresswoman Ruth Bryan Owen, the daughter of William Jennings Bryan sponsored a bill that was passed authorizing the station. (She later sponsored a bill making the Everglades a national park. President Roosevelt appointed her Minister to Denmark in 1933.) However, Public Works funds were not available and it wasn't until 1935 that money was found to begin the project of building the Coast Guard Station. The cookie-cutter design was similar to at least 16 others up and down the eastern seaboard. The station was built on Peanut Island because the first choice location on the lakefront at the northern section of Palm Beach was tied up in litigation and proved to be too expensive. Much of the work

was carried out under WPA contracts. The Works Progress Administration, commonly known as the WPA, was the make work program under Roosevelt's New Deal. Thousands of Public Works projects were used as a means to help the unemployed survive the great depression.

Water wells up to 1000 feet deep were drilled to no avail. A rainwater cistern was used until a water line was run from the mainland in 1938. The boathouse was also built that same year. The station was one of nine Coast Guard stations and one of four designated lifeboat stations in Florida.

*When FPL owned submerged lands (outlined) were to be sold for condo development in the 60s, the Town annexed the area which also included part of Peanut Island.*

For the entire life of the station on Peanut Island, the Coast Guard had the advantage of a quick response to both the ocean and the lake. The drawback was the necessity of having a manned liberty boat available to bring each crewman to the base and the logistics problem of bringing food and materials to the island and removing garbage from the site every day, all of which caused more than just a little cursing. Fuel had to be purchased at commercial marinas for all the station's vessels, which at

*Right Page: Peanut Island as it was in 1954. with the lonely Coast Guard Station. Little Peanut between Peanut Island and the bridge just to north has a good strand of Australian Pine trees. The 1949 bridge is a sturdy concrete structure which replaced the 1935 bridge which sat on wood piles.*

times included two 41-footers, the 30-foot chase boat, and the liberty vessel.

Upon the United States' entry into World War II, the Coast Guard came under command of the U.S. Navy. U-boats prowled the waters of the busy shipping lanes of the Gulf Stream. Twenty-four ships were sunk before adequate forces became available to act as a meaningful deterrent. Five hundred and four survivors were rescued. The four lifeboat stations, along with their civilian auxiliary rescue teams, were the only hope of victims of submarine attacks.

With the Coast Guard Station tucked into its south-east corner, the rest of the island became a tropical wilderness. The growth of Australian Pine Trees covering the slopes of the spoil deposits combined with a continually building white sand beach and sparkling clear waters of the Gulf Stream made this, indeed, a private tropical isle. Couples spent weekends, kids camped out, and many a high school wiener roast took place.

The threat of nuclear attack during the cold war was very real. President John F. Kennedy spent as much time as he could at the family's winter home in Palm Beach. A secret underground shelter was built by the Navy SeaBees on the island adjacent to the Coast Guard Station. The lead-lined concrete and steel structure, completed in 1962, was designed to house as many as 30 people for up to 30 days. It is probably fortunate that it was never needed, as any visitor will tell you that 30 people cramped together for 30 days in that small space wouldn't need a nuclear war to threaten them – they would be at war with themselves within a week. Although island visitors knew about the unlocked shelter, abandoned after the President's assassination in 1963, it was not until 1971 that the government acknowledged the bunker's existence.

*Peanut Island Park Plan 1991. Surviving after threats of becoming a cruise terminal, an oceanographic center, a high rise condo location, and a port parking lot, Peanut Island is now a county park with wonderful facilities for camping, hiking, swimming, and picnicking.*

In 1958 a plan for a bulkhead, which would have extended the island well north of its present boundary, was published. By this time a smaller island had formed to the north and was named Little Peanut Island. The construction of the enlarged Phil Foster Park changed the circulation currents in the lake and, along with the help of a couple of good storms, "Little Peanut" disappeared in the '70s. The bulkheads never materialized.

Word leaked out that Florida Power & Light was going to sell a strip of mostly submerged land that encompassed a small part of Peanut Island. This was of major concern to Palm Beach Shores because of the potential damage resulting from a causeway from the present Phil Foster Park to Peanut Island that had long been talked about. Under the leadership of Mayor Paul Potter, the town began annexation of this strip next to the town's western border. To help justify this move, garbage cans were placed on the island and emptied on a regular basis. The Palm Beach Shores Police Department also borrowed a boat from Bill's Boat Rental and made infrequent patrols of the area.

In 1964 Palm Beach Shores annexed 23.5 acres of the island's 151 acres, which included submerged lands. Two years later the courts reversed the annexation. At least for a short time Palm Beach Shores could claim that it, too, was expanding westward!

In the early sixties a plan was developed that would build a cruise terminal south of and adjacent to Peanut Island. It would connect Peanut Island to the island of Palm Beach. The main channel to the port would go between the island and the terminal via a draw bridge.

*The quiet days of the Port of Palm Beach before and during the World War II. Note the railroad siding. The port was a natural as a terminal for the railroad car ferry service to Havana, Cuba.*

*This 1950 photo shows the port's expansion.which eventually required that the inlet be deepened to accomodate larger vessels.*

Peanut Island would be connected to the area that is now Phil Foster Park by way of a causeway and to Mediterranean Ave. in Palm Beach on filled land. This plan never got off the ground, but over the years there seemed to be regular reports of a new idea to develop Peanut Island commercially.

In 1969 the Palm Beach County Commission took Palm Beach Shores by surprise by approving, in principal, a causeway from Riviera Beach to Peanut Island and then a bridge to Palm Beach Shores. John D. MacArthur, who had just completed his expanded Colonnades Hotel in Palm Beach Shores, was originally thought to be the culprit behind the project. Apparently a gentleman by the name of Adolph Lewson had leased Peanut Island from the Port of Palm Beach and planned to build an oceanographic center. The proposed new causeway and bridge would replace the plans for widening the existing two-lane Blue Heron Bridge and provide direct access to Mr. Lewson's development. Palm Beach Shores Mayor C.J. Wolfe called for an emergency meeting. The commissioners vowed to fight the proposal since they all agreed that a state road bringing traffic into town would have a very negative impact. A similar plan proposed in 1965 was opposed by Palm Beach Shores residents and defeated, keeping a bridge out of their town and retaining their peace and quiet. The oceanographic center never materialized.

Ultimately, the new 65-foot high Blue Heron Bridge was built in 1975.

The Coast Guard, suffering the problems caused by being located on the island, tried once again in 1976 to find a mainland location that was adjacent to the inlet. First, they approached the City of Riviera Beach to purchase two acres of land at the City Marina. The City Council refused to consider the sale. The second choice was in Palm Beach Shores. At the time, Sailfish Marina consisted of only the south dock. What is today the center dock was a separate marina called Bill's Marina and Boat Rentals. The two lots to the north of Bill's were empty and the Coast Guard made an offer to purchase Bill's Marina with these two lots for a price of $850,000. Once again the town was taken by surprise. Not much else was talked about for awhile.

A special town meeting was called. Residents seemed to favor the purchase by a margin of 2 to 1, but the commission voted 3 to 2 to keep the Coast Guard out of town. Loss of future property taxes was the overwhelming reason for the decision. The Coast Guard could have forced the purchase had they wanted to. However, the station commander explained that they did not want to move anyplace where they were not welcomed. They looked at other private property in Riviera Beach and West Palm Beach. One deal fell through and one site near the port being considered was taken off the list because of its closeness to the manatee communal bathtub at the FPL plant. The idea of USCG vessels on an emergency rescue mission having to stop or proceed at dead slow speed to avoid sleeping manatees was not acceptable. The Coast Guard remained on Peanut Island until 1995 when they moved into their present facility north of the Blue Heron Bridge in Riviera Beach. After 59 years, they finally had their home on the mainland, even though they ended up further from the inlet then they would have liked to be.

David Roach, the Assistant Director of the Florida Inland Navigation District, presented plans on April 24, 1991 to the Port Commission for Peanut Island that would make three quarters of the island into county parkland. This plan for a passive park, defined by the state as one without provision for athletic activities such as baseball or soccer fields, was hailed as the first good plan presented for the island. Over the next few years the appearance of the landscape changed drastically. The Australian Pines were removed and the mountain of spoils sand were taken away during a two-year night and day operation. Campgrounds, hiking and walking trails were created, a Ranger cabin was built and hundreds of palm trees were planted. The formal opening of Phase One was held in 1999 and the Phase Two dedication took place in 2005.

The empty Coast Guard facility was turned over to the county. It was leased to a group wanting to establish it as a Maritime Museum. Donations and taxpayer dollars were spent to make some progress, but, while the main floor was being used as a museum, it was discovered that the rest of the facility was being advertised as an exclusive, $10,000 membership fee, private club that would feature a dining room, bar and overnight accommodations. The public outcry put an immediate end to the club, but the museum survived, although after many years, it continues to struggle.

Peanut Island is owned by three separate entities: the Port of Palm Beach; the Florida Inland Navigation District; and Palm Beach County. Today it is a gem sparkling in the crystal clear waters of Lake Worth.

With ample space set aside for the islands main purpose of storage for dredging spoils, there is adequate space for the public park featuring campgrounds, fishing pier, a protected snorkeling area, palm tree lined hiking paths, picnic areas and boat docks, all under the watchful eye of a fulltime resident Park Ranger.

Peanut Island today is a modern day example of what can be accomplished when different government agencies act together for the best interest of their constituents

# Inlet

Today, four inlets connect the Intracoastal Waterway with the Atlantic Ocean in Palm Beach County. Jupiter and Boca Raton Inlets are natural occurring openings whereas the Lake Worth Inlet, also known as the Palm Beach Inlet, and the South Lake Worth Inlet, also known as the Boynton Inlet, are man made.

The Palm Beach Inlet, once created, defined Singer Island and gave Palm Beach Shores the uniqueness of which it can proudly boast. Having water frontage on three sides makes it almost an island unto itself. It also made access possible to

Inlet 1924 view shows the sand build up on north side of the inlet and loss on south side after 6 years of inlet existence. Building on beach is Singer's Blue Heron Hotel. Shoaling in inlet was severe. Maintained depth was 16 feet in 1924.

world class Atlantic Ocean sport fishing less than ten minutes from the town's marinas and is the cause of the island's ever-growing beautiful beach. It has the reputation of being one of the safest inlets in South Florida.

*The Havana Railroad Ferry was started in 1946 by the West India Fruit and Steamship Company.*

Since travel and goods conveyance were primarily by boat in the early days, it made sense that means of accessing the ocean would be very desirable. In the early 1860s August Lang, reportedly the first white resident in the area, dug a trench through the sandy ridges separating the lake from the ocean. This permitted the lake's fresh water to flow into the ocean, lowering the lake until it reached sea level. The flow, created a usable inlet at a location approximately where the one is located today. The resulting inflow of tidal saltwater resulted in a major fish kill in the lake. Between the time when the original trench was dug and 1877, the inlet was constantly closing due to sand build up and had to be worked on every few months and after every storm. The course of the channel would change and at one time ran from the location of the pump house at the ocean to the Flagler Bridge of Palm Beach.

By 1877 the population of settlers around the lake had grown and the need for ocean access became greater. A group met to consider the best course of action. At first it seemed that the easy way was to clean out Lang's channel, but the committee came back with a recommendation to move the channel further north where an outcrop of dead reef rock could be used as a natural jetty. This would help control the erosion and filling that consistently closed previous channels.

The new location was a great idea as far as using the rock outcrop as a jetty, but it also meant that the task ahead was Herculean since it required the moving of 20-foot high sand dunes before digging a channel over 300 feet in length. This was still preferable to just clearing the drifting sand shoals across the low landscape of Lang's original location. Nineteen volunteers showed up initially and more joined them as the work progressed. It took several months of clearing the hammocks, hauling away trees and digging the sand using only shovels and wheel barrows to prepare for the big moment. When they were finished and when the sea wind and tide conditions were favorable, the last few feet were dug out and a rush of ocean water flowed through the new inlet.

For the next 12 years the settlers kept the inlet open, although with a continual build up of sand on the north side the ditch continued to migrate south to the point that the coral rocks were eventually left behind and their use as a jetty disappeared. By this time the settlers were dependent on the inlet to move perishable goods out and bringing store goods in.

By 1889 the depth had diminished to an unusable level and the locals decided to start at the coral out crop once again, only, to make it bigger and better this time round. And they did! According to a newspaper report The group of volunteer workers "created an inlet on a grander scale than anyone at the time had dreamed. When they finished, the new inlet was more than 100 yards wide."

It still suffered from shoaling, but it was being used more than ever in 1893 when Henry Flagler had it enlarged. Again in 1905 Flagler offered to contribute funds to have it reopened after severe weather closed it. In 1912 local officials requested help from Washington, but were denied.

A plan for the modern day inlet started with the chartering of the Lake Worth Inlet District in 1915 by the Florida Legislature. The name was later changed to the Port of Palm Beach District and is usually referred to as the Port District. In 1916 the voters overwhelmingly voted to open the inlet and to have it maintained. The gentleman who had successfully reversed the flow of the Chicago River, Isham Randolph, was hired to survey the area and to select the best site for an inlet. He recommended the present location, which was, for all practical purposes, the same location that August Lang had chosen 40 years earlier.

In 1917 the channel was opened with a depth of 4 feet and protected by two short jetties. Two years later the main channel was widened to 100 feet and dredged to a 10-foot depth. In 1920 the channel was dredged to 12 feet and the jetties extended. Dredging occurred again in 1923, this time to 16 feet and the jetties extended further. Farms to the west of the coastal communities were growing during this time and regular shipping into the lake was seen as a commercial necessity to help get their produce to market.

Proceeds from a bond issue were used to enlarge the turning basin.

A bulkhead, slip and other facilities were built, including railroad and highway connections. In 1925 the first oceangoing cargo ship was welcomed into the port and the following year the first passenger vessel arrived. The Canadian steamer SS New Northland began regular service from the port to Nassau and Havana. In 1926 General George Goethals, famous for his building of the Panama Canal, was contracted to be the consultant for further port and inlet expansion. However, when the bank holding the port's funds went belly up in 1927, work on the inlet stopped. The Waldeck-

*Besides the beautiful scenery walkers on the Parkway are entertained by the regular ship traffic.*

Deal Dredging Company out of Miami completed dredging to a channel depth of 18 feet and removed 60,000 cubic feet of rock from the mouth of the inlet. The area was hit with the county's most severe storm — the 1928 hurricane — followed by the start of the depression in 1929. The Florida boom turned to bust and, like the rest of the country, the area stood still.

From 1929 until 1935 no work was performed on the inlet until the Federal Government stepped in, assigning the maintenance of the inlet to the Army Corps of Engineers. The Corps negotiated with the landowners adjacent to the inlet and were given easement rights, which Mr. Edwards, the town father, inherited when he purchased the southern part of the island in 1947. This easement encouraged the owner (the town) to develop the easement area into a park. It has taken seventy-one years, but as of the beginning of 2006 it appears like it will finally be a reality.

By 1946 The Army Corps of Engineers had restored the jetties, complete with concrete caps, widened the channels, enlarged the turning basin and dredged to a 20-foot depth. The port was not considered a high priority for the war effort and it was not until 1948 that maintenance dredging was performed. Twenty-seven feet was now the new controlled depth.

In 1946 the famous train ferry was established by the West Palm Beach-based, West India Fruit and Steamship Company. Regular service to Havana, Cuba was provided during the early years of Palm Beach Shores development. Due to the lack of homes, residents four and five blocks from the inlet would enjoy a cocktail on their patio as they watched the big ship come and go.

The Port of Palm Beach has always welcomed U.S. Navy ships to visit and hold open house, or perhaps more correctly, open ship. The mid-fifties seemed to be a time when these visits peaked. While the port was too small to handle the first ships of the line, the smaller vessels were constant visitors and many Palm Beach Shores families gave sailors a brief reprieve from onboard life by providing a home cooked dinner and family atmosphere. A few of the ships from that period of time were: the Amphibious Assault Ship USS Rankin; Small Force Transport USS Ruchamkin; Minesweeper USS Nightingale; and Submarine USS Medregal. The largest group visit was by five minesweepers at the same time in August of 1957. The civilian large ship inlet users included Onassis' yacht and President of the Dominican Republic Trujillo's "Presidente."

In 1965 the Corps proposed a further deepening of the channel to a depth of 33 feet.

*After 1967 the inlet, with a controlled depth of 35 feet saw small boat and large ocean going freighter/tanker traffic.*

This was opposed by town residents who were concerned with potential damage to their homes from the dynamiting of the coral bed rock. The dead reef that runs from the east side of Palm Beach and can be seen at the outcrop where the 1887 inlet was built is very prominent at the present inlet. Some of the old buildings, in town, sitting above the reef, still carry cracked foundations from the 1965 deepening of the inlet. A class action lawsuit ended with many residents collecting cost of repair damages.

A larger concern was raised by the residents of Palm Beach who had been loosing their beach since the inlet was originally dredged. The deeper the inlets the more disturbance in the south drift of currents carrying sand to their beach. The arguments presented were at the time legitimate. The only vessels to benefit with a 33-foot draft would be the tankers delivering bunker fuel to the Florida Power & Light plant in Riviera Beach. If FPL would switch to natural gas there would be no need for the deepening. Good argument, but all to no avail.

The year 1967 saw the dredging completed to a depth of 35 feet.

The dredging did not stop the Keva Ideal, a five hundred foot long freighter from running aground in July of 1967. The Keva Ideal was carrying 15,000 tons of cement. She hit a sand buildup just at the inlet's entrance and sat there for 18 hours before being pulled free by three tug boats. She later entered port under her own power and unloaded at the Ideal Cement plant next to the port in Riviera Beach.

In 1978 the 500-foot tanker the Esso Brisbane loaded with 5.6 million gallons of oil and drawing only 32 feet, ran aground at the mouth of the inlet. Luckily the Exxon owned ship was not damaged, but an oil spill barrier was deployed just in case. Sure enough, as

*The increase of the depth of our beaches is in sharp contrast to the loss of the Palm Beach beach on the other side of the Inlet."*

*Even with the deepening of the channel the Keva Ideal ran aground in 1967 and the Esso Brisbane loaded with 110,000 barrels of oil, destined for the FPL plant, did the same in 1978.*

predicted many years earlier, the tanker was attempting to deliver 110,000 barrels of oil to the FPL plant. The ship en route from Venezuela touched ground at the south side of the entrance, just inside the jetty. She swung around until the bow was pointed right at the Town of Palm Beach Shores.

Two local tugs were unsuccessful in breaking her loose and an ocean going tug was requested from Port Everglades. High tide occurred at 4 pm the next day, at which time the Brisbane was floated and continued on her mission. The 40 crew members and all the town residents breathed a sigh of relief.

Maintenance of the inlet is still a full-time chore.

As at all inlets located on the east coast of Florida, the interruption of the close to shore currents causes a buildup of the beaches on the north side and a loss of beach on the south side. Palm Beach Shores has gained hundreds of feet of prime beach while Palm Beach has suffered a great loss. Some mitigation was seen in 1958 when a sand transfer plant went into operation. A pump house located just north of the north jetty sucks up a mixture of sand and water and delivers it across the inlet onto the beach at Palm Beach. The 1957-58 cost to install the pumping station was over a half million dollars. The original pipe across the inlet rusted out in 1990. Since the pipe had caused many problems over the years, especially with the regular inlet maintenance dredging, it was decided to use a pipeline put in place with directional boring that would sit 15 feet below the bottom of the inlet.

This was accomplished in 1996. The sand transfer plant was also upgraded to a pumping rate of 7,200 gallons per minute which translate to a sand transfer rate of 250 cubic yards per minute. 220,250 cubic yards of sand were transferred from Palm Beach Shores beach to the beach along Palm Beach in the year 2000. Sand is also currently trucked from this same location to replenish lost beach sand on the north end of Singer Island. The amount allowed to be moved is very strictly controlled so as to not exceed the amount of new build up. While these actions keep the beach depth relatively constant near the jetty, there is still continuing beach buildup further to the north.

**After all, Palm Beach Shores is still growing!**

*With crystal clear waters the inlet, with an incoming tide, is a divers heaven.*

# Sewers

Sanitary sewers are an important part of the history of Palm Beach Shores. The problem of adequate sanitary sewers festered for more than 30 years before a working solution was found. At least one mayor, two commissioners and members of the Planning & Zoning Board left or were voted out of office due to this issue.

The town was designed, as were all such developments where sewer service was not available, to utilize septic tanks and accompanying drain fields. The topography of the island is such that homes built in the interior of the development were built on land higher than that found in some isolated spots in town and definitely higher than those lots on the perimeter. Most homes were occupied by only a couple and many were used only in the winter season. During normal weather everything worked as planned, but during periods of heavy rain, when the ground had absorbed all the water it could hold, the systems filled and overflowed. Toilets backed up and in some areas a real health hazard existed.

The problem was more evident the further west homes were located from the center of town. The lots on the west side of Lake Drive had the lowest elevations, hence the highest ground water levels and were, therefore, the most problematic. This area was also home to two restaurants.

The Colonnades Hotel had severe problems, described in detail in the Colonanades chapter. The Mayan buildings, on Ocean Avenue had installed a lift station when built in the early '70s, that connected to the Riviera Beach sewer system.

The first major discussion of installing sewers in town took place shortly after the town was founded, in December 1954. The first elected three-man commission voted to make sure homes were less prone to flooding. They mandated, as one of the first code amendments, that building sites must be 12-16 inches above the crown of the road. At the same time, they authorized a study to find ways to alleviate the storm water run off problem, specifically on Lake Drive.

*This 1957 announcement was premature by almost 30 years.*

As the town grew, more properties were affected and in July of 1960 a letter from the Town Commission solicited comments from the citizens regarding possible options for solutions. These included connecting to the soon to be expanded Riviera Beach system with an installation cost of $300,000 (for the whole town) and a monthly charge paid to Riviera of $3.20 for a single bathroom residential home. Additional bathrooms would be charged at 75 cents each. Another choice would be to pay for an intown treatment plant and a third was to construct an off-shore out fall. Whatever the response was is unknown, but no formal action was taken. The problem persisted and in 1965 the Planning and Zoning Board spent considerable time studying the matter and, with the help of professionals, submitted a plan to the commission that was quite unique.

The first local municipality to install a town-wide sewer system was Palm Beach; the second was Riviera Beach. The original Riviera Beach system did not cross the lake and, when it did expand, Palm Beach Shores residents were apprehensive that they would be paying for more than their share if they connected to the new system.

The 1965 P&Z plan was to feed the town's waste via four force main pumps to a fifth larger station that would use a 10-inch force main line across the inlet to Palm Beach. Of all the discussions to date, this plan was the most thought out and all the details were explained. Total cost $525,000.

One of the limiting factors in paying for any type of system was that the town's charter dictated that any bond issue pay interest of no

*Ground Breaking for new perimeter sewer. Bank Manager Bill McDonald on the left came through for the town when original financing fell through at the last minute.*

more than 4%. A good rate in 1949, but not so good in the 1960s. In July of 1968 both houses of the Florida State Legislature passed a bill allowing the town to change the charter. In a referendum in December the voters endorsed a change in bond interest rates to a maximum of 6%. In early 1969 Riviera Beach gave permission to the town to tie into their expanded system, but at a high cost. They proposed the town pay for the cost of their own system and then pay the city $164,000 up front and enter into a 30-year contract. The monthly rate would be the same as what Riviera Beach residents paid plus an extra $3 per bedroom. Another referendum was called for and the town was literally torn apart with those who did not have a problem, not wanting to foot the very expensive solution of a town wide sewer installation. However at a raucous meeting on October 14, the commission voted 3 to 2 not to call a referendum on the question.

The mayor and town clerk could not agree on the minutes of the October 14th meeting. The October 20th meeting minutes reflect that "during the discussion period, there was heated arguments from the audience." A special meeting was called four days later to review the minutes of the October 14th meeting and to consider the conduct of one of the commissioners at the October 20th meeting.

The situation was ugly!

While this was happening, a heavy amount of rain fell, resulting in more tanks overflowing and more complaints. Edward "Ridge" McKenna lived with his wife on Bamboo near Lake Drive. They had small children and the family was forced to use the bathroom at the public beach, all the way across town. Finally having had enough, Ridge took action. First he rented a Port-a-Potty and placed it on his front lawn, not behind the house. This move produced the result he desired by attracting the media and the coverage by the newspapers intensified. The second action he took was to circulate a petition demanding a vote of the town's property owners as to a simple "yes" or "no" to sewers. The petition was signed by 260 of the 440 registered property owners. The commission was forced to call a special election on February 11, 1970. Of the 430 homeowners who showed up, 212 voted "yes" and 218 voted "no." At the regular election in March, the mayor and two commission seats were up for grabs. A team representing the pro sewer crowd won and a newspaper article quoted newly elected commissioner Norris Norman as saying, "the election was a clear victory for sewer proponents."

The problem continued. A commission discussion was held with regards to the town installing its own sewage treatment plant. Plans were supposedly drawn up, but no mention of them officially appears in any available document. The big question of where the plant would be located was never answered. By 1980 there were more homes and commercial establishments in the town and the number was growing. While the majority of homes had no problem, most apartments and motels, which were located on the perimeter streets, had a serious problem that was getting out of control. Having a septic tank continuously overflowing at the height of the season, when the building was full of tourists, was more than just a nuisance for an apartment owner.

The Buccaneer and the Sailfish restaurants were becoming more popular and it was a common practice to have a tank pump out truck stationed on location for the busy Friday and Saturday evening dinner hours. The town solicited help from the Palm Beach County Health Department, but while they recommended a sewer system, they did not insist on one.

In 1980 the problem was worse than ever and the mayor called a meeting of those on the perimeter streets of Lake Drive and Inlet Way. He proposed an engineering study to determine the cost of a system for those streets only. A positive response led to a collection of seed money and a promise from those in attendance to raise the money for the study. Bill Fleming, a resident on the west side of Lake Drive who did not have a major problem himself, volunteered to lead the fundraising. The engineering firm of Barker, Osha & Anderson was used and costs were minimized since this firm had conducted a similar survey years earlier.

A ballot was distributed to the properties of concern looking for financial commitments once the total costs were known. This ballot also explained the details of the proposal and the cost to each homeowner. An equitable cost for each property was calculated by the then Town Manager and building official Robert Crosby. Bob was a soft spoken, self-educated, civil engineer. He took pride in personally double checking engineering drawings and calculations from wind shear to tensile strength for every plan he approved or denied.

He determined the density allowance for each lot. This density, or number of units permitted per acre of land, limited the number of bathrooms allowed on the system from every lot. This, in turn, determined the size of the piping and the capacity of the lift and force main components. It also protected the town from future overbuilding since it locked each lot into a maximum number of units based on the sewer capacity. If anyone wanted more on the lot than the density allowed, he must first obtain a variance and then incur the expense of increasing the sewer capacity size.

Ninety-five percent of the residents affected said they were in favor and pledged to support the project. The system was designed with two lift stations ... one on Ocean Avenue that could handle the eastern half of the town and one on Lake Drive to handle the western half. The laterals were big enough for all of the cross streets to empty into them in the future and the force mains capacity was also adequate for future expansion. The installation was completed without many hitches. A low interest loan was promised by the local Barnett Bank Manager early in the planning stage, but when it came time to sign the contract their Jacksonville headquarters reneged. It looked like the project might have to be cancelled, or at least put off for a year. At a weekly Rotary Club meeting, the mayor told his sad financial tale to Town Attorney Al Everard and Bill McDonald, President of the First National Bank of Lake Park, a brand new bank in the area. An outline of a legal document acceptable to all was agreed upon before lunch was over. Mr. McDonald completed the details immediately, which included guaranteed very low interest loans for residents who desired one, and the project went ahead on schedule. The total cost was borne by the property owners on Lake Drive and Inlet Way.

Mr. Crosby was not a well man during his total tenure with the town and during the sewer installation he was once again hospitalized. A local contractor and officials from neighboring communities were used to carry out the daily inspections, but on more than one occasion town staff filled in. One citizen came into Town Hall and wanted to know what Town Clerk Barbara Weigel was doing in the sewer line ditch with a measuring tape in her hand, dressed in office attire complete with high heels and hose. The nonchalant answer was that she was just checking the run over rise of the new sewer line. Nearly 30 years after the Town Commission first addressed the problem, the solution was found for the lowland septic system problems. Everyone seemed happy since only those who needed sewers got them and those that did not, did not have to pay.

Twelve years later, in 1995, Florida mandated that all homes be on sewers and the town complied. The state also made available low cost loans for this purpose and the town availed itself of these funds.

Although an expensive project, it was a bargain for the residents being added to the system. Not only had the engineering, lift stations, and force mains been paid for years earlier, but the surplus funds from the original installation never got returned to the Lake Drive and Inlet residents. Instead, after the five-year loan was paid off, the excess money ended up in the general fund. Although the sewers are now taken for granted, a few residents still remember the years of bickering when a stand for or against sewers determined the winners of town elections!

# Marinas and Lakefront

Lakefront lots in Palm Beach Shores were the standard 75 feet wide but deep, attracting individuals who built upscale homes to go with the beautiful water view. Some of these homes have since been replaced with mega-mansion style homes, however, many of the original dwellings remain and continue to command admiration from visitors.

In some cases a replatting was done causing a combination of lots or, for example, converting 5 lots into 4. The waterfront lots on the south end of Lake Drive were among the first to be developed. When a zoning map was drawn, these homes were incorporated into the residential district (current Zone "A", two stories maximum). The homes built north of the Sailfish Marina were built after the zoning was established and lie in District "C," which allows hotels and buildings up to three stories. This put pressure on the owners of these properties between 2002-2005 to sell their homes. However, often overlooked is the fact that, when they were replatted, deed restrictions where placed on the lots, limiting construction to one story and the use to residential only.

Mr. Edwards' plans to have a Yacht Club for residents did not last too long. His 1950 brochures promised club membership availability to each property owner in his new subdivision. The Yacht Club amenities included two docks with dockage for 72 boats; 36 located at the south dock where Sailfish Marina is located; 36 at the north dock at what is now Cannonsport Marina. The clubhouse, now called the Buccaneer, included a restaurant, bar and a ship store. It was advertised as the spot where all the locals came to unwind. It definitely lived up to its new reputation as it became the focal point for luncheons, dinners, dances and social functions, as well as the local gossip center for the new town.

Mr. Edwards had reserved for himself all of what later became town owned lands. These parcels originally included the marinas shown as "reserved" on the original plat. Records show the sale of both properties in the early 1950s. The North Dock was operated as the Palm Beach Shores Docks (1951). The second owner changed the name to Doty's Dock (1955). In 1956 Captain Frank Doty applied for a building permit to build a four unit apartment building on the "reserved" parcel of

*Roy's Boat Rentals, located about where the Ship's Store at Sailfish Marina is today, rented small boats for lake exploring and fishing. Later called Bill's Sailfish Marina, not to be confused with the next door Sailfish Center.*

*1947 Dock Construction. Top picture shows building of North Dock (Cannonsport). Bottom shows completed North Dock and not quite finished South Dock (Sailfish). At this time roads were being built but the town looks pretty desolate.*

his land. The town officials denied him permission and it was not until 1959 that the State Supreme Court ruled against the town declaring that a building could indeed be built. The apartment never was constructed because Doty sold the property to George Cannon, who built a first floor marina facility with a second-story apartment as a family home (1960). George called the place Cannon's Port and operated the marina under that name for 19 years. George ran a tight ship and did not allow any trespassers. One story has him stopping Florida Governor Claude Kirk from coming ashore and participating in a heavy discussion with him. He developed a great reputation, of providing a private yacht club atmosphere, among boaters during his tenure.

When the Mills family purchased the marina in 1979 they operated it under the name of Cannonsport Marina and Resort for another 26 years. For that quarter of a century, it operated at capacity and was home to some of the finest sport fishing yachts on the east coast. The property expanded over the years to include the lot to the south as well as three lots to the north. In 2004, after the Marina suffered serious damage caused by hurricanes Francis and Jeanne in the same year, it was purchased by the Realty Division of Nationwide Insurance Company. For all of its life, this marina was operated as a private entity unlike the Sailfish Marina, which welcomed the public with a restaurant and a large fleet of charter boats.

Well known personalities made Cannonsport their favorite boating get-a-way to escape the public eye. The marina staff would dutifully collect photos of NASCAR top race driver Dale Earnhardt seated in his famous number 3 Chevy and have them waiting for him on his arrival, which he would always graciously sign. It seemed that this was one secret that could not be kept. Fans that tried to visit would be ushered off the property, but those who requested permission were told "no" and then offered a personally signed photo if they left their name, phone number and how they wanted the photo signed. Country western singing star Alan Jackson did the same thing. Jackson also made sure the proprietors had great seats for his local concerts. In return, the marina insured their guests privacy by insisting that only boat owners and crew had access to the dock.

Captains and mates determine the success of a marina. They look for a stop while traveling where they know they will be welcome. Privately owned sport fishing yacht crews must travel far from home for extended periods of time. The northern boats coming to Florida for the season favored Cannonsport because it was a family affair. They knew everyone on a first name basis. Regular cook-outs were held with the proprietress' rum cake gaining a reputation from the Florida Keys to New England. There was almost always one captain or mate who was left on the dock when all the others went home for Christmas. They would be invited to join the family for dinner on the one day of the year that the marina was closed.

The Cannonsport Invitational Fishing Tournament was one of the first in the area to promote catch and release fishing. This system allots more points for a bill fish (sailfish, marlin, swordfish, etc.) that was released than for one killed and brought back to the dock to be weighed. The tournament grew in size and prestige until the number of entries had to be capped. Although the prizes were better than other tournaments (Waterford Crystal for lady winners) it remained a fun, honor system contest. The awards dinner was always a highlight, which started out as a home cooked roast beef meal, topped with the famous rum cake. After that, it was held every year at Bill Bonnette's Hunting and Fishing Lodge. Bill's place was on a gravel portion of Hood Road when he hosted the first tournament. By the time the last tournament was held, he was surrounded by developments and the hunting part of his business was long gone.

When country western radio personality Arthur Smith brought his KDW Tournament (Kingfish, Dolphin, and Wahoo) to town, it turned out to be the largest fishing tournament on record. Held at Phil Foster Park, it became impossible to weigh all the fish at that location when the entrees reached 800 boats, so Cannonsport became the weigh in center for large boats. For a long time, it became the one time each year when the dock was overrun with fishermen, TV cameras and reporters. Still, it was not unusual to hear long time town residents exclaim that they never knew Cannonsport existed.

Cannonsport was also the official fueling depot for the U.S. Coast Guard vessels stationed at Peanut Island. In 1979 the fueling was spread among local marinas with the

*View of Cannonsport Marina before hurricanes Francis and Jeanne.*

Sailfish getting most of the day time sales. The fact that Sailfish Marina was using dock girls not dock boys and that most of the Coast Guard crews were young guys, probably had something to do with this.

After regular marina hours there was only one place to buy fuel and that was Cannonsport where the proprietor lived on site. He would be awakened at 2 a.m. and again at 4:30 a.m. to fuel the small Coast Guard boats, only to observe the Coast Guard's large patrol boat fueling at the Sailfish Marina at 9:00 a.m. When he brought it to the attention of the Coast Guard Station's Commanding Officer, orders were posted

*Cannonsport after hurricanes - more than a million dollars in damage.*

instructing that all fuel in the future was to be purchased at Cannonsport. It turned out to be a great arrangement for both parties that continued for many years.

When the boats came in for fueling a little after 1 a.m. day after day after day, it was originally thought that a special operation was in effect until it was discovered that a new "order of the day" was issued allowing all crews having an operation that kept them out past 1:00 a.m. to miss the next morning's reveille. They may have been able to sleep in, but the proprietor of Cannonsport still had to rise at the break of day, every day.

The Coast Guard's District Rodeo was hosted by Cannonsport one summer. Six stations sent their boats and crews for serious competition and inspections, but also to have some fun. The highlight was a water bike competition between base commanders, who all ended up in the lake. After 18 years of coasties coming and going with their spouses and kids, numerous Change of Command ceremonies, and more than one retirement party, the marina's owner's relationship with the Coast Guard came to an end when a new station on the mainland in Riviera Beach, complete with their own fueling depot, opened. The Palm Beach County Sheriff also kept one or two boats at Cannonsport that operated around the clock, which added to the security. Both the Customs Department and Border Patrol also used the marina for fueling, especially when conducting late night surveillance operations.

The 2004 sale of Cannonsport was the end of 53 years of it being the only "mom and pop" marina in the area. Future plans call for a second dock, which will bring the total of large yacht slips to 50. The uplands will be the site for five buildings, each with at least 6 water view condos.

The Sailfish Marina story is a little more complex. Early on, Mr. Edwards south dock was known as the Colonnades dock and when the hotel was sold to the Bahia Mar organization and the hotel's took on that name, the dock became known as the Bahia Mar Yacht Club dock. The Colonnades Yacht Club (Buccaneer) also changed its name to the Bahia Mar Yacht Club. The lot immediately north of the "reserved" parcel at the Sailfish Marina was sold in 1949 to Ralph Warner, who rented small outboard boats to both tourists and locals for lake fishing and exploring. His manager, Roy Henderson, ran the facility as Roy's Boats. In 1953 Bill Bachstet and Ed Roehrich, both early developer/builders in town, purchased Roy's Boats. Ed also owned and operated his family's hardware business, Park Center Hardware on U.S. 1 in Lake Park. They later changed the name to Bill's Sailfish Marina shortly before Bachstet bought out Roehrich. He operated his small boat operations until 1957, at which time he installed piling to accommodate four large boats for charter fishing boat use.

The original sport fishing charters were out of Palm Beach and operated by northern captains as a winter income. As more local owners got involved, they attempted to extend their season by finding businessmen customers instead of just tourist. West Palm Beach City Docks then became the popular dock location. Due to the use of outriggers, the very tall poles that keep fishing lines from tangling, these boats could not clear the draw bridge to Palm Beach and many times had to use valuable charter time waiting for the bridge to open, prompting a move north of the bridge to the 8th Street Docks, also in West Palm Beach. With charter boat popularity growing, the next move was to obtain a competitive advantage by being closer to the inlet. Layton's Dock, where the cruise ship terminal is currently located, was the next home of the local charter fleet.

One unfair competition problem was due to the fact that charter dock owner's usually ran a boat themselves. The first four charter captains to arrive at Bill's Sailfish Marina came knowing that no competitor could claim to be closer to the Gulf Stream fishing nor would they have to compete with the dock owner for customers since Backstet had promised not to get into the charter business himself.

The newcomers were Captain Frank Ardines and his well known boat the "Sail Ahoy"; Captain Al Nathan with "Wendy II"; Captain Bob Rast and his "Commanche"; and Captain John Thomas' "Joker."

When Bachstet expanded his dock to a length of 150 feet in 1966, other charter boats joined the fleet. From then on Bill's was the home to the largest charter fleet in the area. Bachstet sold the property to Lou Perini in 1973. Perini also bought the vacant lot abutting the Buccaneer north of Bill's.

Mr. Edwards sold his interest in the south dock while it was known as the Bahia Mar Dock and the name was changed to the Sailfish Center. It changed hands several times. One of the owners, Lew Parkinson, who ran his own charter boat named "Charmer," sold the property to two teamster officers, a Mr. Meyers and Charles Lynch. Mr. Lynch ran into trouble with the town in 1969 when he replaced the seawall as part of the marina enlargement.

Although a permit had been obtained for the seawall work, no cleats were shown on the permit drawing. This was pointed out to Mr. Lynch, but knowing that the building official was on vacation in Canada, he went ahead and installed the cleats. There is no record as to why the town thought it necessary to play hardball, but they certainly did. Mr. Lynch was hauled into Municipal Court and Judge John Witt fined him $350.

Lynch's reaction was, "I've had it! I'm selling the Sailfish Center and all my holdings as soon as I can and moving back to Philadelphia."

He kept good his promise and sold the marina to town resident Ted Koby, who operated it until 1977.

In 1973 the Manager of the Sailfish Marina was Captain James "Bud" Smith, who is a walking encyclopedia of local waterfront lore. The following year he ran the Sailfish Center, along with his son Tim. Bud started working as a dock boy when he was 8-years-old for his dad, who ran the old West Palm Beach City Dock at the foot of Clematis Street. He

*View of 1970's waterfront. Sailfish Marina has two docks. One in forground was originally known as the 'South Dock' later to be called Sailfish Center. The second dock is the 3rd iteration on Bill's Sailfish Marina. Both later combined to become Sailfish Marina and Resort. Short dock is the Buccaneer and in the background the North Dock later to be Cannonsport Marina.*

obtained his captain's license at age 15 and in the early 1930s ran Harold Vanderbilt's private boat while also chartering his own 34 footer. Captain Bud ferried Mr. MacArthur up the lake to look at the land he eventually bought, which is now MacArthur State Park. Captain Bud's colorful career remains a work in progress.

George Mergens and Alex Dreyfoos bought the Sailfish Center from Koby in 1977. They owned Photo Electronics Corporation (PEC), a company that made a high definition electronic photo processing system they had developed. Their holdings included the local television station WPEC TV Channel 12 in West Palm Beach. That same year they bought Bill's Sailfish Marina and the empty lot to the north, creating a conglomeration that would become a destination location for fishermen and non-fishermen alike. When Bruce Witherspoon leased the little coffee shop on the property in 1979, he turned it into the most popular eating establishment on the Island. By the mid 1980s it became commonplace to find long lines waiting to get into the place for lunch and dinner. Bruce concocted the now famous "Grouper Dog," fish filet fingers on a hot dog roll. This delicacy has been a mainstay of the Marina's Thursday Night Sunset Celebration since its inception.

A third dock was built and the charter boat fleet increased to twenty-five, prompting the Sailfish Marina to advertise having the largest charter fleet in Florida. With all the amenities available to their customers, it became home to some of the larger area fishing tournaments, such as the West Palm Beach Kiwanis Tournament, which has used the marina for decades.

A 2003 newspaper story reported that WCI, a large developer, had purchased the Sailfish for $30 plus million and planned to demolish the restaurant to make way for condos. The news got an immediate public reaction and a "Save the Sailfish" campaign was started. Palm Beach County even took an official position to save the marina. At the time the county was strenuously trying to purchase land to keep water access for small boaters. Launching ramps were fast disappearing and boat trailer parking was in very short supply. The county used the Sailfish as a poster child for a $50 million bond issues referendum to be used for water access. The referendum passed.

WCI backed out of the deal. The marina complex was sold to Brother's Realty, a division of Great American Insurance Company, for a reported $27 million. The buyers agreed to maintain the status quo for two years to allow time for the county to generate a plan. It was determined by appraisers hired by the county that the loss to the owners would be about $22 million if they had to retain the charter docks, the marine store, and the restaurant instead of replacing them with private boats and condos. In 2005 all parties agreed on a $15 million settlement and a deed restriction was drawn up that guaranteed public access to the dock and restaurant.

The new owners, represented by brothers Steve and Victor Fuller, have shown themselves to be easy going with an extremely pro-town atitude. When the town considered having its own fire rescue unit, the Fullers offered to donate $100,000 for a life support unit and they were one of the first to commit to a donation to the new Community Center of over a quarter million dollars.

The Buccaneer was one of the very first buildings in town and the original watering hole favored by town residents. It has been known as the Colonnades Yacht Club and the Bahia Mar Yacht Club before the name Buccaneer finally stuck. It was the scene of daily late afternoon parties when the charter boats at Sailfish finished for the day. The Seasiders would hold luncheon teas. Dinner and dancing was the weekend attraction.

A major parking problem existed from the time the lot to the south was sold and fenced off. Seventeen apartments were part of the original bar and restaurant building. In the 1970s these apartments were remodeled and sold as condos. The bar and restaurant became condo #18. At this time a group of partners, headed up by brothers Frank and Ed Murray, spent a large sum of money upgrading the bar and dinning area. The result of their work, especially the expensive woodworking, has been a source of admiration ever since. Up until then, it was common for a high number of calls to be made for police to respond to disturbances, fights, and conflicts at the establishment on a regular basis. In addition to the investment made to upgrade the physical appearance of the Buccaneer, a concerted effort was made to eliminate this undesirable clientele.

Satisfied that he had accomplished his goal, Frank Murray invited the mayor for a preview when the work was finished. After the tour, as he proceeded to proudly tell the mayor how they had gotten rid of the riff-raff, one of the patrons sitting behind Frank out of his view, but in full view of the mayor, quietly passed out, slipped off the high bar stool, and gently landed on the floor!

The upgrade did not keep the boat crews out; in fact, they really liked the new upscale atmosphere. In truth, the bar had depended on them for years and without them a financial crisis would probably have ensued.

The Sailfish next door also had a bar, but proprietor Bruce Witherspoon felt his limited seating was better used by his early-bird diners, so he had no real objection to the competition. The owners of the Sailfish did not necessarily agree with Bruce and at one time planted a barrier of very large plants as a barricade so close together that no one could walk through. This meant Sailfish crews had to walk out to the street and back into the "Buc" bar instead of the few steps they previously walked from their boats. One morning, like a scene from "Mister Roberts," the plants nearest the water were mysteriously found swimming in the lake, thereby re-establishing a walkway between the two businesses. The plants were immediately reinforced with razor wire and the town had to step in and have it removed. The "Buc" was known as the home of the boat captains and crews from all the marinas until it closed.

The new owners of Sailfish Marina purchased the bar and restaurant condo. With their new Sailfish Restaurant next door, the owners made a decision to use the Buccaneer for banquets and special occasions only. For the first time in over 40 years the "Buc" did not have a parking problem!

# Parks

Not many towns can boast of parks that stretch from border to border in an East to West direction and also North to South. Thanks to the foresight of the developer, Mr. A.O. Edwards, the original plotting included a north-south parkway which dissected the town. It ran from a fountain and balustrade entry at the north end, all the way through the town to the inlet. There it met the east-west running easement dedicated to the U.S Government for the inlet maintenance. According to the 1935 easement document the strip of land adjacent to the inlet was to be restricted, but a park was specifically called out as a recommended use.

An area at the beach was also designated for public use and included enough space for a parking lot for beachgoers. These areas formed the basis of the park system known today but the land, when given, was not exactly what is seen today. The town brags about its citizens volunteering for many projects, but none can compare with the original "Chain Gang." This group of husbands of Seasiders (the women's group in town) along with members of the Property Owners Association put in thousands of hours, first in building a seawall to separate the parking lot from the blowing sand from the beach and then to build the Pavilion (demolished in 2005 to make room for a new Community Center after serving the residents for over 50 years). Next they formed and poured a sidewalk the length of the town and planted trees and grass to turn the sandspur infested walkway into a park to be proud of. Most of these men worked full time and gave up their weekends, over many years, to make these projects happen.

The one fault to be found in Mr. Edwards' planning was made was when he sold his waterworks to Riviera Beach. He also sold the land that the water tank and pump house was sitting on. The 300,000 gallon water tank and the pump house sat adjacent to the Town Hall complex. Over the years the Walkway became a beautiful park, but its Town Hall Center became a storage area for Riviera's construction debris. In 1985, the city gave permission, allowing the town to "beautify this area" and a fundraising program began. The local Rotary Club donated benches and the Exchange Club installed their famous Freedom Shrine. This is a display of historic documents from the Articles of Confederation to the World War II signing of the Japanese Surrender.

A fountain was installed and waterworks apparatus disguised with fieldstone façades. Stakes were put in place and chicken wire attached so that the vines that were planted would grow to hide the water tank. Plants and trees were planted and sod put down after a sprinkler system was installed. A meandering sidewalk was formed and poured by the two public works employees, and assorted volunteers. Even the driver of the cement truck took pity on the amateur crew and got into the mess to help. The best picture of the day was when Sergeant, now Captain, Steve Kniffen reported for duty looking spiffy and dapper in his highly polished shoes. He made the mistake of letting the crew know that he once worked in construction and had finished cement jobs many times. The sun was going down and the concrete was beginning to set. Steve was cajoled into proving his expertise. By the time the sergeant finished the job, he was a hero, albeit a bedraggled hero with shoes that shone no more.

A dedication ceremony was held with as well as a congressman, state and county representatives along with the Mayor of Riviera Beach. The Sheriff's Honor Guard, a pipe band, VFW members, good weather and a great crowd made the day a huge success.

This scene was to be repeated in 2003 when the obsolete waterworks and the land were purchased from Riviera Beach and the tank removed, the pump house converted into offices for the Police Department and the area professionally redesigned as a park. The new design included removing the Public Works garage entrance from the side to the rear thereby freeing up the space between the Town Hall and the Police and Fire Hall. After the remodeling which included a gazebo, grassy knolls, trees, plants and flagpole, this section of the parkway became the showpiece of the park.

In the 1950s the beach was flat from the water's edge to the parking lot. The "Chain Gang" had poured a sidewalk from the lot to the lifeguard stand (which the lifeguard was required to sweep each day). Volunteers created the original dunes, not to prevent erosion, but to keep the sand from sandblasting the cars in the parking lot. By the '90s the state had mandated dune walkovers and one was built accordingly (one less job for the lifeguard). In 2003 a landscape area was added as well as a children's playground. The cost of the playground was split three ways with the town paying a third, the Rotary Club of Singer Island a third and the local Kiwanis Club a third. The original seawall was replaced with a cut stone seawall and picnic tables installed under an umbrella of newly planted palm trees.

A celebration combining the dedication of the beach park and a new fire truck for the Volunteer Fire Department was held with a cookout attended by many of the citizens.

The inlet area has been difficult to bring up to the standard of the Parkway for a number of assorted reasons. First, there is the consideration that this area is prone to storm damage on an annual basis. Second, since the town has not maintained this area in former years the encroachment by adjacent property owners has resulted in well maintained lawns that are treated as private property. The idea of using taxpayer dollars to develop this strip when the results could be negated by the next hurricane would not be a prudent one. Within two years and with $370,000 in grants from state and county, ground was broken for phase one of the improvements. This included paver brick walkways, gazebos, retaining wall, sprinkler system, low level walkway bollard lighting and provision for heavy equipment access to the beach and the sand transfer plant. All designed to still be in place after a major storm, even if they were covered by a few feet of sand!

The parks at Town Hall, the beach and the inlet were paid for with grants from the state and the county. These grants were the result of the work of Town Administrator Cindy Lindscoog.

The parks are one of the main reasons the title of "Best Little Town in Florida" can be claimed.

*The Parkway, running the full lenth of the town, is the centerpiece of the "Best Little Town in Florida.*

*Town Hall area used for Public Works.*

*Same area after removal of water tank and creation of park.*

# Events

The events held in the town over the years have been the glue that binds the community together. From the very early days the Seasider's afternoon teas and dinner dances presented the opportunity to meet a neighbor. The Seasiders have always had their special interest groups and one called the Four Arts Group Committee conduct visit and tours to galleries, museums and concerts for members and guests. The Community Service Group meets weekly to prepare crafts to be given as gifts to the needy or to be sold to raise monies for charitable causes. A Garden and Beautification Committee worked the Town Parkway while the Social Affairs Group had functions ranging from Halloween parties to Christmas decorating celebrations. All of these brought the town together in a spirit of commonality.

Similarly, for years the biggest event in town was the annual Property Owners "Spring Fling," a dinner with dancing held at the beach pavilion. Themes for this BYOB bash have included Western, Pirate, Roman, Greek and come-as-you-are dress. Prizes for the best costumes made for some hilarious fun provided by the more adventuresome attendees.

One of the most meaningful events has been the recognition award given to citizens who have performed outstanding service to the town. The Property Owners Association began this award at a special dinner meeting held at the Sailfish Marina restaurant in 1999 and later incorporated the award ceremony into their annual "Spring Fling." The original recipients were Barbara Sanderson, Hank Gardner, Marty Kastner and Bruce Witherspoon.

The Christmas Party, also sponsored by the Property Owners, is still a gala affair that is well attended although not as strong as in the '70s and '80s when more than 300 people crowded the Colonnades Ballroom.

The Fire Department's picnic was a not to be missed good time. This event featured games, including the popular egg throwing contest. Held on the Colonnades property in the 70s it was the group's main social event at that time. An afternoon card playing party has been hosted at the Town Hall meeting room for many years by the Ladies Auxiliary. This is an excuse for ladies to have a luncheon and to spend the afternoon visiting seldom seen friends and acquaintances. This, of course, is especially true for the snow birds.

The bicentennial celebration in 1976 was not forgotten in Palm Beach Shores. Besides the formal ceremonies, the firemen painted every fire hydrant in town to look like miniature minutemen. They were a topic of conversation of residents and visitors alike for many years.

A plan was hatched in 1982 to hold a celebration to get everyone out of their homes to meet each other. This idea was thought necessary since many new families had moved into town. The budget was tight and using tax payers' dollars was not a possibility. The employees answered the call and raised seed money for the event with a community car wash. It was quite a sight to see the normally business office attire and police uniforms replaced with shorts and swim suits and high heels with flip flops. The event, under the guidance of Commissioner Bob Widman and advertised as a Town Birthday Party, was a great success, filling five blocks of the Parkway with antique autos, petting zoo animals, stage shows, a Punch and Judy show, pet contests and an amateur talent show, as well as thirty crafter's booths and a golf match at an upscale golf course to determine the Town Champ. The

*An event not to be missed is the fundraising Pancake Breakfast put on by the local Rotary Club and the Property Owners Association.*

Birthday Party changed its name for the second year to "Fun Fest," a play on the name "Sun Fest," which was being widely promoted as South Florida's biggest celebration. Commissioner Hank Gardner and Retired Air Force General George Sylvester, with the help of a group of two dozen volunteers, headed up the event for many years. It continued to grow for eight years before finding volunteers became a problem to carry out the hundred of hours necessary to insure success and a lack of full support of town officials surfaced.

In 1986 the land just north of Town Hall was owned by Riviera Beach as part of the water system and used for many years as a storage area. It was without a doubt the most unsightly part of the otherwise beautiful Parkway.  When permission was granted by Riviera Beach officials for the town to maintain the area a beautiful transformation occurred. A new park was designed and included a Freedom Shrine sponsored by the Exchange Club of the Northern Palm Beaches and benches from the Singer Island Rotary Club. These features were located near a meandering circular sidewalk. The 300,000 gallon water tank was camouflaged by vines growing up the chicken wire that surrounded the tank. On dedication day officials of Riviera Beach, Palm Beach Shores, both service clubs and both the local Legion and VFW units joined the crowd to watch the pipes and drums of the Sheriff's Band and Color Guard march into the park. State Representative Marian Lewis was the dedication speaker. Approximately two hundred people joined in the celebration.

In 2001 a year long 50th Birthday Celebration was carried out under the Chair of Commissioner Josephine (Jo) Gosline. It kicked off with a pancake breakfast in January; a black tie dance (in conjunction with the Singer Island Rotary Club) in February; a  parade in March, complete with a 3-tier birthday cake float.  It continued with an event each month for the entire year. The 4th of July fireworks on the beach were described by literally dozens of people as being the best ever seen. The finale was to be a New Years Eve Bon Fire on the beach. The 31st proved to be a day of continuous rain and a decision was made to postpone the event until the next night. The fire engine was sent through town informing the citizens of the change in plans and anyone who showed up was told to come back the following night. Sometime late that night some revelers saw the monstrous pile of wood and threw in a flare. Even though the wood was wet it not only burned, it also spread to the stockpile and all the driftwood that had been collected over a period of months went up in flames. The next day officials were caught in a

The Town's 50th Birthday was celebrated with a year long schedule of events. The icing on the eight foot high cake looked good enough to eat. Commissioner Jo Gosline and her committee gave us a party that won't be forgotten.

Nationaly televised The Town of Palm Beach Shores hosted beauties from all over the country at the 1968 College Queen Beauty Contest held at the Colonnades Hotel.

"nothing to burn" dilemma. At the time the remains of three Tiki hut structures were on the beach. They were not in good shape and were constantly filled with sand. A quick decision was made for them to become the bon fire material and the show went on as planned. The event was a huge success with the whole town joining in the fun. Not only was the weather great but a full moon came rising out of the ocean to make things picture perfect.

A plan that was presented in 2002 for street lights, crosswalks and traffic calming circles in town was received by some in a very contentious manner. People generally dislike change and this was to be a major change. It was decided to have a small scale example of the project and funds were allocated for such an installation. One block on Tacoma was designated and ornamental street lights were installed, a traffic circle at Atlantic was built and a pavers cross walk at the Parkway completed. Then a "Taste of Tacoma" celebration was announced. Town folks were invited to stroll the blocked off area and to vote on which improvements they liked and would be willing to pay for and to enjoy music and an ice cream social. Once again the Town Hall staff got into the act and manned (or womanned) the soda, ice cream and voting booths. The resulted tally showed lights and crosswalk being approved but the turning circle just barely having a majority in favor. As a result of this event, the

*Mayor Paul Potter brought local municipality leaders to the Colonnades for a charity Cow Milking Contest. Won by Riviera Police Chief Lennie Cottrell.*

*The Easter Bunny makes his regular appearance at the Town Hall Easter Egg Hunt.*

town, within a year, had financed and installed streetlights on every street and crosswalks at the Parkway's street crossings.

The 2003 ribbon cutting, celebrating the completion of five major projects in town (sidewalk on Ocean; sidewalk on Lake; street lights, crosswalks and dedication of the new park located at Town Hall had the record for most big wigs in attendance which includes a County Commissioner, State Senator, State Representative, Federal Congressman and Environmental officials. All had a pair of scissors in their hands.

A challenge was issued for a bed race by the City of Boynton Beach and the town answered. The preliminaries were held beachside at the Riviera Beach Mall and the Palm Beach Shores entry was without a doubt the best design of the day. Not only did it look good but this engineering marvel, powered by recruited unsuspecting town jocks, beat the US Army entry. The Army team tried to impress the crowd by doing push-ups before the race, but it apparently had the wrong effect and just tired them out. A support group of citizens, attired in town T-shirts, cheered on the victorious team. Unfortunately the home team declined to enter the finals held in Boynton saying they could not handle any more crowd adulation.

The event that took the longest period of time from conception to ground breaking ceremony was that of the Community Center.

The idea of such a center was first announced in 1982 as a worthwhile project. Ground breaking was finally a reality in January of 2006. The difference in cost? Planned cost in 1982 was less then $250,000. Projected cost in 2006 was $2,000,000. Volunteer Firefighters cooked hot dogs and hamburgers during the groundbreaking celebration. A great bon fire on the beach was scheduled to be the finale of the evening. More than 300 meals were served, but the winds were so strong that the fire had to be postponed for safety reasons. Milly Male, who was a commissioner and Vice Mayor in the 1980s, was present and participated in the ground breaking ceremony and was without a doubt the most excited person in attendance. She was a strong advocate for the Center for many years and was thrilled to see that it was becoming a reality.

An almost "official" town event and without a doubt, one of the most popular, is the St. Patty's Day Parade. This happening started out with a few good Irish residents celebrating the way any good Irishman would by having a few drinks and holding their own parade. The idea

*The Mayor's Youth Council directed by Police Lt. Steve Langevin conducts activities for kids including an annual Halloween Dress-Up Party.*

was a popular one and the next year a little more organization went into the planning. Years later it is the largest annual event that the town sees. The parade is so long that the beginning units are returning to the staging area, which is also the judging stand, before the last unit has started. From antique autos to the multiple Shriner units; from Mounted Policemen to highland bands; from local elected officials to county commissioners and state senators, this parade has it all.

Events that were not planned but certainly affected the town were named Francis, Jeanne and Wilma. Although the town suffered from hurricane damage over the years, nothing in its history left the marks that these storms did. The loss of trees and other vegetation from Francis was still being cleaned up when Jeanne hit. The structural damage to lakefront, the decimation of the Parkway, the loss of the Tiki structure at the beach cross walk and the obliteration of the inlet walkway area from these two storms took years to restore.

*The 2004 hurricanes left their calling cards all over the town.*

*St. Patrick Day Parade is the town's "unofficial" largest annual event.*

# History 1940s

The landscape that Mr. Edwards saw when he scouted the island for his next development was one of sand dunes, beaches and scrubland. There was a sparse growth of Australian Pine along the lakefront and at a few other locations. The strip that is now the Parkway supported some scrub, but, for the most part, only sand and sandspurs greeted him. Singer's original bridge to the island had been washed out in the 1928 hurricane and was not rebuilt until 1935. The new one, like the old, was set on wooden pilings and consisted of wood planking. By 1946 the pilings were half the original size, having been eaten away by wood worms, and the planks were loose. Driving across this long span was not for the faint of heart.

Mr. Edwards was not daunted by what he saw. Instead of the blowing sand he envisioned streets and homes; instead of scrubland he saw parks and gardens. He is given credit for the actual layout of the town. His vision included a tourist driven perimeter and a single family center core. The development extended beyond the present northern boundary, and the Plaza area was designed to be the town's retail strip mall. The original plan contained 631 lots. The oceanfront lots were planned with a building set back that guaranteed a minimum of 100 feet of open beach. Since the beach north of the jetty builds up over time, the planned open beach space is much greater today. Ocean Avenue and Lake Drive followed a path approximating the contours of the waterfront. A private beach, 356 feet wide by 150 feet deep was dedicated to town residents. Two 300 foot docks were planned and access roads to the inlet, the beach and the docks are shown. The Parkway running from a planned entrance featuring a fountain at Bamboo and continuing all the way through town to the inlet was included with the exact dimensions it has today.

Besides being a visionary, Edwards was also a very astute businessman. Once he had committed and bought the 200-acre tract from the Inlet Investment Corporation for $475,000 he put infrastructure, roads, docks and hotel construction simultaneously into fast mode. He also pressured the state and county to readdress the bridge access problem. He

*'40s Steen Beach House. Ryder Steen's Eatery was the first establishment on the island and lasted more than a quarter century.*

purchased land at the corner of Blue Heron and A1A, adjacent to the Florida East Coast Railroad where he sank water wells and built a water purification plant. He ran water mains from that location to the present Town Hall site where he installed a 300,000 gallon reserve tank and pump house. He made arrangements for two experienced workers, William Messer and Harold Wasner from the West Palm Beach Water Works, which at that time was a private company, to work for him on their off time, supervising the installation of water lines to each lot.

He also began a marketing campaign to let the world know of his "Island in the Sun." By 1947 plans were released in a sales brochure showing an artist's conceptions that were generally accurate, but it also included a full-color town plan which was identical to today's map. Photos show the paved streets completed and fire hydrants installed. Only one unidentified, just under construction, building is depicted. The brochure played up the beach, four golf courses within a five-mile radius, many tennis clubs and sport fishing only five minutes away and the fact that the island was right next to Palm Beach. All of these accomplishments were completed in less than a year from signing the purchase agreement.

Sales began before the tract was recorded with the county. In September of 1947 Lots 464, 488 and 489 were sold to C.A. Fleischer of West Palm Beach. What is interesting is that the deed includes four legal size pages of small type "restrictions." These restrictions were the basis of the town's present day Code. While many have been revised over the years, it is still possible to find those that contain the identical language of the original deed restrictions. Items covered included Use of Land, Nuisances, Signs, Unkept (unkempt) Lots, Docks, Building Set Backs and Open Spaces, Plan Approvals, Easements and Septic Tanks.

As an example of the farsightedness of Edward's deed restrictions in 2005, the Planning and Zoning Board recommended that bow, or protruding windows be allowed to project into the set back area. The original 1947 deed restrictions read, "Single story bay, bow and oriel windows may encroach not more than 3 feet into the set back area, but not to exceed a total of 30 square feet along any one side of the building." Maybe the wheel can be reinvented!

In 1940 the officials of the town (not yet a city) of Riviera Beach were chastised for purchasing a plot of land on the ocean. The City of West Palm Beach had just recently refused the same offer. After all who needed to buy beachfront when there were so many miles of open beaches all around? However, when development on the island began, the beach came into focus. The Palm Beach Shores project extended north of Blue Heron Boulevard leaving the beach belonging to Riviera cut off from the rest of their town on the mainland. A court determined that a line should be drawn along the south side of the

*Town in 1947. What the island was like at start of construction. Peanut Island and Little Peanut Island. No homes in north end of Palm Beach. Bend in road went west to Old Wooden Bridge 400' south of present bridge location. in front of bend is Steen's Restaurant.*

**REVISED PRICE LIST OF LOTS — FEB 1 1952**

**PALM BEACH SHORES**

Office on Island
Turn East at Riviera Beach
Over Singer Bridge

City Office — 213 Fern St.
West Palm Beach, Fla.

| Numbers | Price | Numbers | Price | Numbers | Price | Numbers | Price | Numbers | Price |
|---|---|---|---|---|---|---|---|---|---|
| 10 | 3,300.00 | 383 | 4,000.00 | 436 | 2,500.00 | 465 | 1,500.00 | 535 | 8,750.00 |
| 12 | 3,300.00 | 384 | 4,000.00 | 438 | 2,500.00 | 468 | 6,000.00 | 536 | 8,750.00 |
| 13 | 3,300.00 | 385 | 3,300.00 | 439 | 2,500.00 | 469 | 2,750.00 | 537 | 8,750.00 |
| 14 | 3,300.00 | 386 | 3,300.00 | 442 | 2,500.00 | 470 | 2,750.00 | 538 | 8,750.00 |
| 19 | 3,300.00 | 387 | 3,300.00 | 444 | 2,500.00 | 471 | 2,750.00 | 580 | 8,750.00 |
| 20 | 3,300.00 | 388 | 3,300.00 | 445 | 2,500.00 | 472 | 2,750.00 | 583 | 8,750.00 |
| 47 | 4,000.00 | 389 | 3,300.00 | 446 | 2,500.00 | 473 | 2,750.00 | 584 | 8,750.00 |
| 48 | 4,000.00 | 390 | 3,300.00 | 447 | 2,500.00 | 493 E | 2,000.00 | 585 | 8,750.00 |
| 49 | 2,800.00 | 395 | 2,800.00 | 449) B | | 493 F | 2,000.00 | 586 | 8,750.00 |
| 91 | 2,800.00 | 397 | 2,800.00 | 450) | 3,000.00 | 493 G | 5,000.00 | 587 | 8,750.00 |
| 166 | 2,800.00 | 402 | 2,500.00 | 450) A | | 493 H | 2,000.00 | 588 | 8,750.00 |
| 198 | 2,800.00 | 403 | 2,500.00 | 450) B | | 493 I | 2,000.00 | 589 | 8,750.00 |
| 208 | 2,800.00 | 404 | 2,500.00 | 451) | 3,000.00 | 493 J | 2,500.00 | 590 | 8,750.00 |
| 224 | 2,800.00 | 405 | 2,500.00 | 451) A | | 493 K | 2,500.00 | 591 | 8,750.00 |
| 225 | 2,800.00 | 406 | 2,500.00 | | | 493 L | 2,750.00 | 594 | 15,000.00 |
| 239 | 2,800.00 | 409 | 2,750.00 | 451) B | | 493 M | 5,000.00 | 595 | 15,000.00 |
| 250 | 2,800.00 | 410 | 2,750.00 | 452) | 3,000.00 | 497 | 2,750.00 | 596 | 15,000.00 |
| 257 | 2,800.00 | 411 | 2,750.00 | 452) A | | 499 | 3,190.00 | 597 | 15,000.00 |

*Prices were low by today's standards but would still be a bargain. The 1952 $3,300 would be $24,317 today.*

beach border and that line should be continued in a westerly direction into the lake to Palm Beach Shores' western boundary. South of the line would be Palm Beach Shores. North of the line would be Riviera Beach. The developer did not really care. Since he still owned the land and since Riviera Beach did not have any other developments on the island, there was no confusion to his customers. However, when Palm Beach Shores was chartered into existence, problems arose. Most of the residents to the north wanted to be part of the town. The arbitrary border that was imposed chopped many properties in two, one part being in Riviera and one part in Palm Beach Shores. Taxes and services have been unfair to these residents ever since. Even constructing a building in this area meant getting two building permits and meeting two different codes with the attendant two sets of inspectors with which to deal.

Before this division took place, Mr. Edwards offered to allow beach parking on his land next to the Plaza if Riviera would pave the area offered. By this time in the fall of 1949 there were establishments bordering the beach who paid rent to Riviera and who needed parking for their patrons as well as the beachgoers. Even though Riviera never did pave the area, Edwards still gave permission for the Plaza area to be used for parking.

One establishment that must be mentioned was that of Ryder Steen and his wife. Steen's

*This 1949 photo shows the new concrete bridge as well as what is left of the 1935 wooden structure beside it. Little Peanut Island, the North and South docks, paved streets, the Inlet Court Hotel and very few completed homes greeted visitors at this time.*

*1949 bridge completed. Remains of old wood bridge still visable. Streets and docks and first homes can be seen. New bridge is 400 feet north of old one on island.*

Restaurant on the Riviera Beach property, was considered the first commercial establishment on the island. They were also early and long time residents of Palm Beach Shores. The only recognizable building on the conception drawing in the town's first sales brochure is that of Steen's. With a magnifying glass his name can be made out on the wall of his restaurant. That drawing showed the proposed new bridge, the two docks and the oceanfront hotel, although it is not mentioned in the text. The hotel is shown well north of its actual location and the Town Hall is shown on the wrong side of Edwards Lane.

By March of 1951 half of the lots numbered 1 through 50 had been sold. By December of that year 41 of the 50 were bought. The prices had only increased slightly from the original price list, as Mr. Edwards had promised; interior single family lots $2,700; lakefront and inlet $8,700; oceanfront $15,000.

The focal point of the Palm Beach Shores development was to be the oceanfront hotel named by Edwards as the Inlet Court Hotel. The construction was started in 1948 and early photos show the hotel under construction with a foreground of beautiful new roads covered in many spots by drifting sands.

By late 1949, the time of the second sales brochure publication, enough construction had taken place for photos, not drawings, to be

'40s Beach Promo. Mr. Edwards had to import people to get this early brochure photo.

used. Full page ads were also taken out in major newspapers, including the Miami Herald in February of 1950. Photos of completed buildings at Cascade and Ocean, Atlantic and Sandal, Ocean and Blossom, featured the Romaine on the Inlet and the beautiful new $1,500,000 Inlet Court Hotel with its Olympic size swimming pool. The county completed a new concrete bridge a few hundred feet north of the old wooden one, removing one of the major objections of potential buyers.

The second set of ads also bragged that unlike other developments, this one had all of the needed improvements completed and paid for. They claimed that over one million dollars had been spent on improvements to the development in 1949-50 alone. Some of the cost quoted: ten miles of paved roadways $240,000, water system $400,000, docks (2) $70,000. (In 2005 it cost well over a million dollars to replace the north dock.)

A special building department was available to assist lot purchasers with planning, building and supervising the construction of their homes. This free service allowed visitors to go north and to have their new home ready upon their return in the fall. The development was F.H.A. approved for the purchase of both homes and apartment buildings. Lots were sold with one-third down and the balance payable over the next three years.

The third iteration of sales information was a full-color brochure that explained all of the recreational advantages of living in the Shores. They illustrated the park entrance with the graceful balustrades, lights and fountain. The hotel's dining room on the ocean, now named the Colonnades Hotel, is pictured with its canvas awning. Mr. Edwards determined that the original name for his hotel, the Inlet Court, sounded too much like a motor court or motel and not a destination hotel. The Colonnades name came, from the series of columns supporting the second floor balconies and walkways.

*Power is on the island and the homes are popping up all over! This is Dr. Marquis' house on Claremont Lane. He had a clear view of the inlet from his patio when he moved in.*

The lakeside docks are featured and show the Yacht Club with a very recognizable view of the Buccaneer Restaurant grounds. The caption read, "One of the finest Yacht Clubs and boating facilities in southeast Florida, is located on the Lake Worth side of Palm Beach Shores. There is a marine supply store, restaurant and lounge, plus dock space for seventy-two craft. This is a favorite gathering place for yachting enthusiasts among residents." The docks mentioned were located at the site of the present day Sailfish Marina (called the South Dock) and Cannonsport Marina (North Dock). The amenities were located at the Club House, which is now the Buccaneer Restaurant. A picture of a cabin cruiser going out of the inlet shows four buildings in the background, two on the ocean, one on the inlet and one inland.

This brochure also had photos of four completed spec homes, advertised as ready-to-move-into.

The transition period when the development changed into a bonafied town was well planned. In February of 1951, 58 residents signed a petition for incorporation. An Organization Committee was established and a referendum election was held on the 27th of the March, "which carried in favor and was approved." The development began its corporate existence as a municipality known as the "Town of Palm Beach Shores" when the ballots were tallied and showed 41 voters in favor and 5 opposed. A three-year period was established that would end with the turning over of all town matters to an elected commission and the complete exiting of Mr. Edwards. When some of the horror stories are told relating to developers who took their money and ran and knowing the early history of the Florida swamp land sales, it becomes clear just how fortunate it was to have a town founder who built a community with an underlying pride of accomplishment.

Sunrise

*What has not changed over the years is the natural beauty of the town.*

Sunset

# A View from Town Hall

## 1950s

In Mr. Edwards' plan to gently ease out of his direct involvement in running the town he proposed a three-year intern period. The Charter directed him to have a mayor along with a two-man commission. He appointed his attorney, Bruce Jones, and his business manager, Sam Morris, to be commissioners. He set up a system of tax assessments, trash collection and all the other essential services that the new development needed totally at his own expense during the first few years. His construction vehicle was used as the town truck, his watchman acted as the policeman, and his employees became the town's trash collectors.

The first zoning ordinance of July 1953 divided the town into three zones. Zone A was single family limited to two stories but without a height limit; Zone B had the same restrictions for single family homes and a three story, 40-foot limitation for multi-family buildings; and Zone C allowed hotels, apartments and clubs with unrestricted height. There was not a separate D Zone. There oceanfront properties were part of Zone C.

Due to a misunderstanding, some residents believed that the first election would be held in 1953 not 1954. They formed a committee within the Property Owners Association, hired a lawyer, and were prepared to sue the town's founder and sitting mayor to force an early election. A letter from Mr. Jones outlining the cost to the residents of such a premature move ended the discussion and voters went to the polls, as planned, in March of 1954. Mr. Edwards eliminated any further controversy regarding local representation by having his two employee commissioners replaced by a Mr. Schultz and Mr. Peerson to serve the one remaining year period before the 1954 elections.

The three new commissioners who were elected determined that the one with the most votes would be Mayor, the runner up would be Vice Mayor and the third would serve as Commissioner. Mr. Henry Peerson became the first elected official to serve as Mayor; Alfred Bohny was Vice-Mayor and Russell Schultz Commissioner. They faced many agenda items as they took office, but their first item of business was to honor Mr. Edwards. He was presented with a rosewood gavel inscribed "A.

O. Edwards, First Mayor of Palm Beach Shores, 1952-54" on a silver band. Although Mayor Peerson had been a leader in the attempt to sue Mr. Edwards a year earlier, he paid tribute to the founder.

"A few years ago a man drove over a rickety wooden bridge," Mr. Peerson said, "looked at a pile of sand and envisioned the Town of Palm Beach Shores. He provided the new community with a water system, the best roads that money can buy and other monuments that attest to his foresight and faith in this area. That man, A.O. Edwards, became the town's first Mayor."

Mr. Edwards, visibly affected by these unexpected remarks, simply replied, "I hope this town will last forever. If there is anything I can do to help, just ask me."

The new commission immediately got to work by introducing ordinances to control signs and mail boxes in town. They heard from the Coast Guard that the petition signed by three hundred residents, objecting to the noisy bell buoy in the inlet, had not only been endorsed by local Congressman Rogers, but that the buoy was to be replaced within two weeks.

In the first year they battled the county's desire to install a pump-house at the inlet. The pump would transfer sand across the inlet to Palm Beach. Town residents strenuously objected to the taking of their sand as well as the noise of the pump. The newly elected officials also had to address the serious flooding problems on Lake Drive and consider the many changes to the Charter that the Property Owners Association was proposing. The new commission soon learned that it was much easier to demand changes as property owners than it was to create change as an elected official. One victory was the sale of a structure known as "the Barracks" to the town for $6,000. This wooden building, adjacent to Town Hall, had originally been used as a construction storage building during the town's early development and had been transformed into a living accommodation for employees of the Colonnades Hotel. The mayor promised to get rid of what he referred to as "this eyesore" as soon as possible. Formal objections were made concerning Riviera Beach's proposal to construct a sewage treatment plant on Peanut Island and to the Port of Palm Beach request to install oil storage tanks at the same location.

In an effort to alleviate future flooding, they established a new building grade minimum level requirement of 12-16 inches above the crown of the adjacent road. They authorized town entrance signs, a 24-hour police station inside Town Hall, a private garbage collection contract, floor covering for Town Hall, the purchase of a utility truck, a water cooler for Town Hall, dog and cat licenses, and called for Civil Defense plans to be drawn. All in all, it was quite a busy beginning!

The citizens agreed to a Charter change in a December 1955 referendum. The change enlarged the commission from three men to five with four Commissioners At-Large and a Mayor elected directly by the voters. As a result, Mr. Peerson became the first elected Mayor in March of 1956. Since this was the first five-person election, all seats were open. The mayor and two commissioners would serve a two-year term and the other two commissioners a one-year term.

The voters also decided bars should close at 2 a.m., instead of the other choices of 3 a.m. or 5 a.m. Two hundred and seventy voters (270) were on the rolls in 1956, compared to two hundred and seven (207) in 1954. Besides Mayor Peerson, the commission included Vice Mayor Beaumont Davison; George Dougan; Wheaton Douglass and Wells Jewett. Town resident Charles Bair was appointed Town Clerk. The town was authorized to conduct its own municipal court and each year a Town Judge was appointed along with a Town Attorney and Town Clerk.

The subsequent growing period the town settled into abounded with loads of activities provided by the ladies organization known as the Seasiders. Picnics, parties, dinner dances, a Christmas home lighting contest, and Chain Gang work projects in the Parkway and at the Beach kept everyone busy. The whole town was involved with the early going-ons. There were only 270 voters registered in 1956 and 237 of them attended the Seasiders Dance that year.

In 1957 plans were made to remove the rear portion of Town Hall and to replace it with a two-story structure. The ground floor would house Police and Public Work vehicles and the second story would have the Town Commission meeting room, a courtroom and the caretaker's apartment. These plans were carried out the next year, Richard Trexler, the town's first

Building Inspector, Plumbing Inspector, Policeman, Mailman, Maintenance Man, Desk Clerk and whatever-else-he-was-needed-for, moved into the apartment while taking a pay cut to offset the free accommodation.

Plans for a $650,000 sewer treatment plant were announced in 1957. Riviera Beach residents on the island were invited to utilize this facility if they desired. The city declined the offer and also declined to enter into any discussion regarding annexation of a small number of city residents adjacent to the town, some having property crossing the border requiring them to pay taxes to both the City of Riviera Beach and the Town of Palm Beach Shores.

The year 1957 saw the election of the two commissioners who had been elected in 1956 for an interim one-year period. From that date forward the mayor and two commissioners would be elected for a two-year term in even numbered years and the remaining two commission seats would be decided every odd numbered year.

Commission meetings, usually described as "exciting as a Southside Knitting Club meeting," exploded on Monday, September the 8th, 1958. The attendees did not agree with the commission's action regarding hiring, without advertising, a building official. Someone who thought they should have been considered for the position hired a lawyer who continually asked leading questions of the commissioners. When the attorney made one particularly

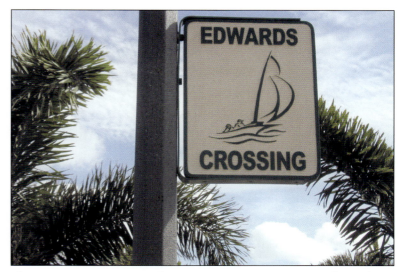

disparaging remark, one commissioner lost his cool and shouted out,"If that goddamn lawyer says one more word, I will pop him in the nose!" The lawyer jumped to his feet and demanded an apology. The two men started to meet in the center of the room. Mayor Peerson ordered the Police Chief to step in and restore order. No dais existed at the time and the commissioners sat at a table directly in front of the audience. The mayor restrained the commissioner and the Police Chief grabbed the lawyer.

After things calmed down an apology was again demanded and given, but not exactly in a civilized manner. When no apology was forthcoming the lawyer shouted, "How about an apology to the goddamn lawyer?"

"Alright, I apologize to the goddamn lawyer!" the commissioner responded.

The gentleman under consideration for the position shouted, "I would not accept the job under any condition," and walked out.

## 1960s

It seems that only negative activities are newsworthy. The next event to make the local news occurred in 1960. Mayor Cox and two new commissioners were elected on a ticket to "clean house." At the organizational meeting in April of that year, three town employees were fired and Mr. Ernest Able was hired to replace them. Mr. Able was an experienced civil servant, having worked for the City of West Palm Beach for many years. What caused the controversy was that all of the arrangements were made outside the Commission Chamber without the knowledge of the other two elected officials. Florida's Sunshine Law did not exist in 1960; it was not enacted until 1967. The two commissioners who found themselves out in the cold left the meeting, as did Planning and Zoning Board appointees who did not agree with this secretive way of doing business. Both of the commissioners stuck it out though and were re-elected again in 1961. Mr. Able stayed with the Town of Palm Beach Shores for nine years.

The 1959–60 Budget was $83,000 with the Police Department accounting for 31 percent of the total amount.

One of the few complimentary newspaper articles started by asking, "How would you like to live in a town without drugstores, sidewalks, grocery shops, garages, service stations and barber shops?" The story proceeded to unfold about the 1,000 residents who loved it. The article extolled the 400-foot beach and the "from one end of town to the other" Parkway.

Town founder A.O. Edwards died. Mr. Edwards owned the beach and Parkway, but stipulated in deed restrictions that they were for the exclusive use of bonefied property owners. With the commission's agreement control was given to the Beach and Parkway Authority. Later Edwards' estate transferred all of his property to the Town of Palm Beach Shores itself, taking the Property Owners Association out of the picture as custodians of any town real property.

In 1963 the town had no height restrictions for waterfront properties. Every owner of such property showed up when the commission discussed putting such restrictions in place. At that meeting Mr. MacArthur, who had a purchase option on the Colonnades property, was turned down in his quest to have the building line on the beach extended an additional 100 feet (it had just recently been extended 100 feet). He announced that without the additional extension he would go ahead with the purchase, but instead of a hotel he would turn the Colonnades into a nursing home, thereby removing the town's largest tax payer from the rolls. The maximum height dilemma stayed on the front burner and a 6-story maximum was placed on all perimeter Waterfront land.

After much controversy, permission was granted to deepen the inlet from 27 to 37 feet. The resultant around-the-clock blasting shook the buildings along Inlet Way. It could even be felt further inland. When cracks began showing up in the concrete block structures, 48 property owners made claims and 34 actually sued. They won some compensatory damages, but not many were satisfied. Fortunately the Great Lakes Dredging Company completed the work by the December deadline and tourists were not disturbed.

Mayor Paul Potter noticed that the rip-rap, the large rocks lining the inlet, was washing out and asked the trustees of Edwards' estate for the reversionary rights to the inlet easement that they held. The dominant easement rights are held by the U.S. Government. With these rights granted, he then approached his contacts at Rubin Construction who were in the process of tearing up Blue Heron Boulevard. The mayor offered the contractor a nearby place to dump the torn up asphalt. The contractor accepted immediately. With this asphalt worked into the rip rap the washout was, at least temporarily, stopped.

Next, Mayor Potter contacted Palm Beach County officials and convinced them that a paved walkway along the inlet would be ideal for emergency vehicle use. Despite objections from some Inlet Way property owners, the walkway was created from the Parkway to the jetty area. The concern was centered on whether or not guests would loose some privacy, but all were happy with the final results. One individual, who objected loudly and promised to remember who was responsible at the next election, showed his mettle as a man when he came back and apologized in front of the commission saying that he and his guests loved it!

Mayor Paul also drew up the legal papers for the establishment of the Volunteer Fire Department. As a member himself, he answered one of the first serious calls when Riviera Beach had a riot and a lumber yard burned to the ground. The new engine was the pride of the town. The men were always happy to show it off, especially in Riviera Beach since the city's demand for an unreasonable high price of fire protection caused the creation of the town's Fire Department in the first place.

## 1970s

The 1970 election was once again about sewers. The mayor and two commissioners were elected as a team, running on a platform promising the installation of sanitary sewers. They tried, but to no avail.

In 1971, Mayor Frederick Muller and two commissioners walked out of a town meeting when a discussion over the enforcement of an ordinance got heated. Trailers, trucks and motor homes were banned from overnight parking in town, but boats were not. The mayor wanted them included and was waiting for the P&Z to revise the ordinance. The

attendees wanted immediate action on trucks. When a stand-still ensued, the mayor asked for a motion to adjourn. He then declared the meeting over and walked out with two commissioners, leaving the other two and the audience of about twenty people discussing the issue among themselves. No enforcement took place before boats were added to the prohibited overnight parking list.

Another discussion took place of an ordinance that required felons to report to the police within 48 hours of coming to town. These felons would be fingerprinted and issued an I.D. card to be kept with them at all times. A similar procedure would be used for non-resident employees, including gardeners, domestics, liquor handlers, nightclub workers, taxi drivers, janitors and hotel, motel, and apartment workers. The reasoning was that a prime suspect list would be available for any crime committed in town. The ordinance never made it through second reading. It was reminiscent of another era. In the 1950s, Senator Joseph McCarthy had the entire nation stirred up over fear of communist infiltration into America. It was common to have the oath of office include the words, "I am not a member of the Communist Party." Also, there was a similar, short lived, law on the books in 1955. Ordinance #23 required all employees of hotels, apartments, clubs and others to register and obtain I.D. cards which had to be submitted to the Town Clerk or Police Department.

The Colonnades Hotel construction was finished. Although problems with the town still existed, most of the furor stemming from the lawsuits and controvery between John D. MacArthur and the local citizens over the hotel had dissipated. In fact, Mr. MacArthur was talked into dressing up as Santa Claus and play host to 50 kids at the Property Owners Christmas Party held at the hotel. Later problems again surfaced when Palm Beach Shores refused to grant an Occupational License and Mr. Mac sued the town for harassment. MacArthur went ahead and rented the rooms anyway.

A Town Commissioner complained about the noise at the Colonnades during construction of a wing connecting the main hotel building with the newly acquired Sea Spray Motel to the north.

A big fuss was made to enact an ordinance to cover the situation. The result was a few faces with egg on them when it was discovered that such an ordinance already existed. However, by the time it was discovered the work was completed.

MacArthur was also charged with polluting the town's swimming beach waters and causing them to be closed for four weeks. The hotel installed a pipe that discharged overflow from Mac's duck ponds and septic tanks. A commotion erupted involving the town, the County Health Department and the hotel, which dragged on with accusations flying in all directions. Test results of the affected waters finally gave the hotel a clean bill of health without any punitive action being taken. The Heath Department had publicly stated that the pipe was the culprit, but could not get enough evidence to prosecute. In the meantime, the hotel stood by its story that the problem was caused by droppings from birds!

Also, 1972 saw the election of the first female commissioner. Millie Male served many years as both Commissioner and Vice Mayor. Thirty four years later, in 2006, she was called out of retirement to help in the groundbreaking ceremony for the new Community Center.

*The grounding and long term visit by the Amaryllis created a deep beach and surfing cove. The Hilton Hotel used the build-up for expansion - temporarily!*

During her tenure she had championed a Center located at the beach. She also spoke up and endorsed a six-month moratorium on building in "C" district while the six-story height limit was examined. The code was later revised to the present six-story maximum on the ocean and three-story maximum on the lake and on the inlet. Norris Norman was a commissioner who voted for the limited height on the lake and inlet even though he was the owner of the Buccaneer and certainly knew he was limiting his future financial gain along with the height.

A year later the Zoning was once again changed, this time creating a forth district. Zone A was defined by the existence of single family homes, mostly on the interior lots but some on the lake. Zone B was non-waterfront apartment / multifamily structures; Zone C the waterfront properties on Lake Drive and Inlet Way; and Zone D all the lots with ocean frontage. The ordinance firmed up height restrictions with two stories being the maximum in Zone A and B, three stories in C, and six stories in D.

The Singer Island Civic Association requested that Palm Beach Shores annex the Riviera Beach portion of Singer Island. After much discussion the town decided against such a move fearing that the 3,700 population in the annexed area would take control of the town residents who would be outnumbered 3 to 1.

Palm Beach Shores had annexed a portion of submerged lands west of the original town's border in the lake, including a corner of Peanut Island, in 1965. This was done to stop a planned commercial development which included apartments being built on filled areas. The developer took the town to court to have the annexation rescinded. His argument was that the town could not support the fire, police or trash collections on the Island. He prevailed and in 1970 the town shrunk back to its original borders. Due to an oversight, the annexed land stayed on the Palm Beach Shores tax role. It was discovered by the tax collector in 1974 prompting a finger pointing battle between Palm Beach County and Palm Beach Shores. It was settled by dropping the land from the rolls for the current fiscal year but not

requiring that the county be paid back the previous year's taxes that the town collected. This resulted in a current year $21,000 budget

deficit, which had to be made up with contingency funds.

The town's budget for 1973-74 was $241,358 and each employee and volunteer firefighter was given a $10 gift certificate as a Christmas bonus.

A court decision in January of 1974 defined beachfront property rights, which would have a long-term effect on the town. The Hilton Hotel, located in Riviera Beach, made use of the build-up of beach sand behind their building and added additional units. This beach build-up was not a normal accumulation, but rather one caused by the grounding of the Greek freighter, Amaryllis, in 1965 when Hurricane Betsy drove the 400-ton vessel ashore. The next year Hurricane Inez drove a former Navy LST that was being used as a salvage vessel on shore as well. These derelicts acted as a manmade jetty collecting sand of the north side while creating a large bay on the south side. The wrecks were finally removed in 1968 and the sand that had built up started to disappear as the beach returned to its old configuration. Without major storms, the Hilton builders were lulled into a false sense of security by the 200 additional feet of sand. The 50-foot addition was built in 1970. By 1972, with a few good storms, the high tides were lapping at the building and a seawall was built to protect it from further erosion. Although the Department of Natural Resources issued a temporary permit for the cofferdam, they refused one for a permanent fixture. The State of Florida also got into the act and would not allow the cofferdam to be maintained. The issue ended up in court for Judge James Knott to determine state and private rights on beachfront property.

The state's position was based on laws dating back to the original settlement of Florida. English common law states that the title to all land below the mean high water line belonged to the crown and held by the sovereign for the use of all his subjects. Therefore, the state claimed sovereignty over water up to the high water mark based on this ancient British law, as well as laws based on early Spanish land claims, all of which is clearly spelled out in the Florida State Constitution.

The court's decision was based on the fact that the public had access to the portion of the beach that was exposed at low tide even though the property owner owned down to the high tide line. If the owner constructed anything between the low and high water marks, it would deny the public access to this land. As a result, the cofferdam was removed, the addition to the Hilton was washed-out by the surf but Palm Beach Shores' public beaches along with all others were protected by one of the most common sense decisions by the court.

At year's end Mayor Bruce Lewis called to convene all mayors of the 37 municipalities in Palm Beach County to oppose the county's $50 million bond issue to purchase beach property. The opposition was based on the county's plan to purchase the vacant land between the Riviera Beach public beach and Palm Beach Shores' beach. The referendum went through, but the town's parcel was dropped from the list. The fact that MacArthur was offering to lease his property on the north end of the island to the county for $1 per year helped to remove public attention from the beach parcel. When the land lease deal failed to materialize, MacArthur donated the land to the state and it is now the beautiful J.D. MacArthur State Park.

In 1975, Mayor Bruce Lewis and Police Chief Wolff quit as a result of political bickering. Mayor Lewis was halfway through his second term. Chief Wolff had served for 19 years. Lewis claimed the new financial disclosure laws was the reason he was stepping down and the chief cited commission interference with his department as his reason. Paul Klang, who was Lewis' political foe, was appointed Mayor and he appointed a new Town Clerk and Police Chief completing a total shakeup in the town's administration.

New Police Chief Robert Roberson was an experienced officer who served as a detective across the inlet with the Palm Beach Police Department. He also served with the Palm Beach Gardens Police Department. He completely revised the Palm Beach Shores Police Department by modernizing procedures and creating professionalism in the department.

Bill Bachstet owned Bill's Marina for 20 years before he sold it to Perini Land Development Corp., marking the end of a fishing era in the area. Bill had the four deep sea charter boats at his small dock and also rented small outboard motorboats by the hour for lake fishing and exploring. Perini also bought the vacant lot to the north, between Bill's and the Buccaneer, and eventually

purchased the Sailfish Marina as well. This created what would be known as the Sailfish Center for the next thirty plus years.

1976 was the year of the American Bicentennial. The celebratration in Palm Beach

Shores was held with a ceremony in the Crystal Ball Room of the Colonnades Hotel featuring State Representative Tom Lewis, a Bennington 13-star flag dedication at Town Hall, and with the fire department painting each fire hydrant in town to look like revolutionary war soldiers.

This was also the year of another major milestone in the town's history with the opening of the new Jerry Thomas (Blue Heron) Bridge. For the first time citizens could come and go without the backed up traffic conditions caused by Mr. Edwards' 1949 two-lane draw bridge.

A lawsuit brought against the builder of the Mayan Towers for faulty workmanship sought $46,000 in damages. The complaint included the need for a pumping system to get usable water pressure to the top floors and a new roof on the less than five-year-old building.

The commission authorized the completion of the inlet walkway from the Parkway west to the lake, including a concrete pad at the lookout area.

The next big controversy was centered around the overnight truck parking ordinance that caused the mayor and two commissioners to walk out of a meeting back in 1971. The ordinance was not being enforced as a number of vocal citizens attending the commission meetings thought it should. The commission agreed and the Police Chief was ordered to crack down. However, a controversy erupted when the commission determined that a "truck" was any vehicle with a truck bed, including an El Camino that parked regularly at the Buccaneer. This vehicle was very stylish and had a regular automobile cab, but it had a pickup truck bed in the back. The commission claimed it was a truck, while others insisted it was an automobile. The town pushed forward with its enforcement crackdown, which led to a long, expensive court case. When the case was decided against the town, the code was rewritten to prohibit any commercial vehicle to park in town overnight. The new code has since been upheld in the courts.

## 1980s

The year 1980 saw the sewer issue taking on a life of its own. The County Health Department had insisted that the Colonnades install a method of connecting to the Riviera Beach system, but the rest of the problem areas suffered from overloaded septic tanks with every good rainfall. The waterfront properties on Lake Drive and Inlet Way were especially prone to backup in season when the motel apartments were full and the restaurants were busy. There was no easy solution. A mandate from the whole town would be necessary for such an ambitious program. Not only did the majority not suffer from this problem, but townwide sewers had been defeated on two previous occasions. A meeting was called for the owners on Lake and Inlet that were affected. They agreed to pay for an engineering feasibility study. They then agreed to pay for the installation of the system that would be built with adequate facilities to handle the whole town if and when they came on board. The system capacity was determined by the allowable density as per the code in effect at the time. This meant that any future development would be limited to that density unless someone paid to enlarge the system. Less than two years from the first meetings, the perimeter sewers were working and both streets were repaved. Plus, it was all paid for by the users.

The town's purse strings were drawn more tightly closed than at any other time in the town's history. The town newsletter "Homeport" was designed and published for almost four years. No direct tax dollars were used. Local businesses paid to advertise in the paper and all the writing, typing, layout, editing and proofing was performed by volunteers. The same situation existed in getting a park built on the property adjacent to Town Hall and owned by the City of Riviera Beach. No tax dollars were available and many expressed the view that nothing should be done to improve non-town owned property. The local service clubs, as well as town organizations, were called on to help, but the majority of funds came from individuals. The result was a public park that became the pride of the citizens, which was described as "making the proverbial silk purse out of a sow's ear."

In 1982 the first Fun Fest was held. The idea of throwing a party to encourage residents to participate and to meet their neighbors was agreed upon, but money was needed to get things started. Town Hall employees, including the police, dispatchers, public works, the building official and the entire female staff, held a car wash and successfully raised the seed money to hold what was called a Town

Birthday Party. It was so successful that the next year it was held again, this time as Fun Fest, and was repeated annually through 1990.

The "Best Little Town in Florida" phrase was first used in 1982. It became the official Town Logo when it was resurrected in 2000.

The mayor was also a volunteer fireman. It was determined that he could not accept the Christmas turkey given to the volunteers each year as it would violate the state's "elected official gift" ethic requirements.

The 1986 election included a referendum that became one of the most important pieces of legislation in the town's code book. The voters approved a charter change that forced any height or lot coverage above 10% of the permissible code to go to public referendum before it could be considered by the commission as a variance. In the next twenty years this provision was used four times: once to encourage a building to exceed the code (Marriott first four buildings) and three times to emphatically recommend no change be allowed (Marriott building 5, proposed four-story condo on west side of Ocean Avenue and again to deny proposed three-stories in a two-story zone).

In 1986 voters elected Palm Beach Shores' first female mayor, Marion Klang. She served for two years. Her husband had been mayor from 1975 until 1980. In 1988 Tom Chilcote was elected mayor and proceeded to lead the town for 12 years. His terms were among the smoothest in the town's history. He ran unopposed for six terms. His main accomplishment included the much needed expansion of Town Hall, without taking away from the appearance of what was the best recognized symbol of the town. There was, however, many minor, and not so minor problems, such as a contractor who didn't pay his subcontractors, forcing the town to step in and pay them directly.

### 1990s

In the 1990s the state mandated sewers for the town. The entire residential community and all others not already on sewers were forced to comply. The state offered a low cost loan to make the project possible without straining the town's budget. A lot of problems would have been eliminated if this had been made available 10, 20 or 30 years earlier.

The "Top of the Hill Gang" saved the town thousands of dollars with their palm tree

*Five of the major projects were celebrated at the same Ribbon Cutting Party. Top ribbon represented the Town Hall Complex Park.*

fertilizing, stop bar painting at street corners, and many other similar chores. As is typical with any volunteer organization, the same individuals ended up doing all the work and they kept getting older. They joked among themselves that the "Top of the Hill Gang" was becoming the "Over the Hill Gang." It became harder each year to recruit able bodied workers, but this attitude of volunteerism that had its roots in the beginning of this little town is one of the main characteristics that sets it apart from others.

Mayor Chilcote was rewarded for his long tenure by having the Town Hall meeting room named Chilcote Hall.

The Embassy Suites, later called the Raddison and finally named the Palm Beach Shores Resort, had been approved with 20% less parking than what the code demanded creating an ongoing problem.

The Marriott came into Palm Beach Shores when the residents were running scared. After sitting empty for years, The Colonnades was finally torn down, leaving the barren property surrounded by an ugly chain link fence to greet visitors to the town's main street. Rumors abounded regarding the future use of this prime property. The strongest rumor had the state opening a mental hospital on the grounds. When the Cunard Steamship Line proposed a 5-star hotel the residents eagerly voted to allow eight-story buildings. Marriott later purchased the development from Cunard and inherited the height variance. They proposed building five new timeshare buildings. In the mid-1980s timeshare was not an accepted ownership arrangement. Its poor reputation was due to developers leaving town with major problems left behind, not the least being empty units with no taxes being paid. An ordinance limiting timeshare to oceanfront property (District D) only had been placed on the books since one time share already existed in District D and, with no other oceanfront property available, it was thought that there could never be another timeshare built in town. When the ordinance passed, no one expected that the Colonnades would meet its demise in the next few years. A committee, headed up by resident Bob Morris, was formed to investigate the Marriott's other timeshare projects. They actually visited the Hilton Head location in North Carolina and came back with a positive report. The developer was given a go-ahead. The result was a renaissance for Ocean Avenue.

At the same time a halfway house moved in, taking the town by surprise. Commissioner Bill Reep startled his peers by announcing that he had sold and/or rented a portion of his apartments to a group that catered to worn out executives. Townsfolk were soon gossiping about the youthful looking worn out executives and their colorful tatoos!

In the late 1990s the town was by-passed while the housing boom expanded west and north. Stagnant home prices actually made it become a low price area. A few residents interpreted this as a sign of non-recoverable decline and moved out of town. At one time, 35 homes were on the market. It was possible to buy a two-bedroom, two-bath home for as little as $129,000. This was comparable to, if not cheaper than, a starter home 30 to 40 miles in the country. The town's location was still the most desirable, there was no crime, and every home was within walking distance of the ocean, lake and inlet. The low prices led to a new trend of young families moving into town at an equal if not higher rate of retirees.

## 2000s

In 2000 a major change in administration occurred. The new officials were elected on a pledge to reverse the perceived decline. The first Marriott building came on the tax roll and the additional tax along with a bank loan and grants from the county and state all helped pay for the improvements that brought the town up to par with other fast appreciating municipalities. Residents enjoyed major land value appreciation along with the infrastructure improvements.

The improvements included: sidewalks on Ocean Avenue, Lake Drive and Inlet Way; a new police annex building; street lighting on all streets; pedestrian crosswalks at all streets along the Parkway; traffic calming circle; new kids' playground; a major renovation of Town Hall; and two new town parks, one at the beach and one at Town Hall.

Along with the infrastructure improvements, the creation of the Mayor's Youth Council attended to the needs of the new families, under Sergeant (later Lieutenant) Steve

Langevin, who also ran the Community Policing Program. A new vehicle was obtained to be used for a Citizens on Patrol (COP) program. A new Fire Engine was acquired for the Volunteer Fire Department. And a very competitive "step" salary program, along with a take-home-car program for the Police Department, was established. A start on the talked-about–for-years Community Center and talked-about-even-longer creation of a park along the inlet were also part of the overall plans for improvements. The plans were successful, possibly too successful. At the peak of the housing/condo boom not only had the real estate values caught up with surrounding areas, they were leading the pack. The 1997 $129,000 home sold for $800,000 in the fall of 2005.

In 2001 the town became one of only three communities in the state of Florida to have their boundary expanded, for Police jurisdictional purposes, 1,200 feet off shore. This was done with the help of Representative Jeff Atwater (later State Senator) with the passing of a special act by the state.

A large amount of redevelopment on the perimeter of town occurred. Some of the oldest buildings in town would be replaced with beautiful designed condos. Most of the buildings being replaced had been used for transients, whereas the new condos and townhouses would attract permanent residents who would, hopefully, have a greater appreciation and respect for the town. Pressure to relax the codes was strong as some believed that developers would not invest with the limited amount of profit that would be made under the stringent codes that existed. Fortunately the Planning & Zoning Board and the Town Commission held out so that the developments taking place depended on quality not quantity to be successful. Voters stated their wishes in a 2002 referendum when seventy-five percent voted to keep the height of buildings in District B to two stories.

The parking problem was still the most visible problem in town. To provide parking on a small lot and build a quality building, within the limited code allowance for height and lot coverage, was difficult in not impossible. Mr. Jery Hunter purchased a lot on the inlet and his architect, Mr. Joe Legan, came up with a scheme that answered a lot of problems. His plans showed that by having the grade level at one foot above the allowable maximum above the crown of the road and then excavating a minimum depth, he could have all the required parking under the building. This allowed maximum building size for larger units and no automobiles in sight while maintaining height and lot coverage codes. This approach was so appealing that the commission allowed a grade level one foot higher than before and all the new multifamily developers followed suit.

New rules and regulations are the curse of smaller municipalities and Palm Beach Shores is no different. Mandated reports, requiring hours of skilled workers time from both the state and federal governments, has required either more inside help or using outside contractors. One example is the N.P.D.E.S. (National Pollutant Discharge Elimination System), an annual report requiring extensive time and use of an engineering expert to complete. Since Palm Beach Shores is built out, with a different storm drainage system not feasible, and since the town does not qualify for federal or state aid with its storm water system, this requirement is nothing more than a very expensive time-consuming report costing tens of thousand of dollars and the threat of big fines and loss of any federal funding for non-compliance.

For fifty years smaller municipalities had the option to use a cash system of accounting, but that option was taken away and an accrual system was required. Not only does this cause more work, but it also presents a financial picture far different than that presented in the past. For instance, when purchasing two police vehicles at $42,000 with payments spread over three years it would, in the past, have been budgeted at $14,000 (the amount paid in the fiscal year). Under the new system, it is budgeted at $42,000 (the total obligation) and that inflated budget must be presented to the public.

A proposed liquefied natural gas line from the Bahamas to the FPL property in Riviera Beach has taken up a lot of effort and financing to keep up with. The original plan showed the line coming in through the inlet, well beneath the surface. While within the town boundary, it did not appear to be a major concern. A second plan surfaced later without any warning of the change to town officials. This plan had the line running directly below the inlet walkway and a boring location on the property. A committee was set up, headed by Vice Mayor Bill Hayes, to come up with a recommendation. The result was to hire a Washington lawyer who specialized in this sort of action. The attorney got a delay and then a suspension of the gas line plans. The current fossil fuel shortages make it a certainty that this issue will reappear in the future.

Another costly incident occurred surrounding the water rates Riviera Beach charged the residents of Palm Beach Shores. Mr. Edwards, who had installed the water system, sold the system in 1951, including the wells and the land both in Riviera Beach and in Palm Beach Shores, to the city for $10. In return the city promised to supply water to the town at the identical rate that they charged their own residents.

When the 300,000 gallon tank, the pump house, and the land they sat on, (adjacent to Town Hall) became surplus due to the installation of larger pipes to serve the island, the town entered into an agreement to buy the property. A price was agreed upon and authorized by both the Palm Beach Shores Town Commission and the Riviera Beach City Council. The timing of the completion of the deal was critical since the town had accepted a grant from the state and from the county based on this agreement. The state grant, to be used to develop a park on the purchased property, required proof of ownership by a certain date or the grant would be cancelled. With only a few days to go Riviera Beach said they were putting the contract approval on their agenda. Approval was granted, but with the stipulation that staff would complete the details. Those staff details (with Riviera Beach's mayor's blessing) included a 25% increase in water rates. When told this was unacceptable they demanded a court decision to determine if the city could force the issue. The matter advanced to the State Supreme Court with the accompanying financial costs to both the city and the town.

Perhaps the problem of most long-term concern is the eroding of "Home Rule." At the time the town was chartered, it was given all the rights to rule itself, having to only worry that its laws did not conflict with state regulations. Counties are subdivisions of the state that give services and protection to areas that are not incorporated. Large wealthy counties, like Palm Beach County, became Charter Counties and given similar rights as that given to municipalities. They have, over the years, stepped on local rights and many attempts to do away with smaller communities in favor of a "metro" approach have been proposed. While getting rid of duplication of services is a worthy cause, the downside for Palm Beach Shores would be a loss of what the town is all about. A metro system could not deliver a policeman to a resident's door within two minutes, which is the norm. Nor would a dispatcher send help to aid a senior citizen to get back in their chair. Fire protection by professionals would probably equal or even exceed the current volunteers' performance, but the fabric of the town that they and their Women's Auxiliary supply would be lost.

As long as they exist, along with the Environmental Committee, the Beach Clean-Up Volunteers, the Top of the Hill Gang, the staff, and the non-paid appointed boards and commission, Palm Beach Shores will be a town where residents and strangers alike, continue to greet each other as they walk along the Parkway, the inlet and the beach, thanking their lucky stars that they are here to enjoy …

**"The Best Little Town in Florida."**